"I am such a fan of this book. Everyone doubts. But not everyone is a great companion in times of doubt. Adam Groza is a phenomenal companion. Why? Because rather than glamorizing doubt, Adam acknowledges the realities of doubt and then points us to the Scriptures and to Jesus who invites us to follow Him by faith. This book will bless you."

—Daniel Fusco, lead pastor at Crossroads Community Church (Vancouver, WA), TV & Radio Host, and author of *Crazy Happy*, *Upward, Inward, Outward*, and *Honestly*

"With the heart of a pastor and the breadth of a philosopher, Adam Groza offers biblical insight and practical advice to readers asking questions like: What is doubt? Why do we doubt, and how does it relate to faith? Can we progress from doubt to faith? If so, how? And how do we help others do the same? Groza is to be commended for this wise and winsome volume."

—Christopher W. Morgan, dean and professor of theology, School of Christian Ministries, California Baptist University; and author and/ or editor of more than twenty volumes, including *Christian Theology: The Biblical Story and Our Faith*; *Concise Dictionary of Theological Terms*; and *Systematic Theology Study Bible*

"Admitting doubt is not a denial of faith but rather a necessary step in developing genuine faith. Every person has doubts—about God, His mysterious ways of working in our world, and our frail capacity to believe in Him despite global turmoil. Facing doubts, rather than denying them, is the path forward to a legitimate, soul-satisfying, intellectually stimulating faith in God. This book is written by a real person who has struggled with doubt and grappled with the reasons for faith. He has come through the process to a profound and settled belief in God and a faith-filled worldview as a result. Join him on the journey to the same destination!"

—Jeff Iorg, President, Gateway Seminary

"Traveling through Scripture, Adam accompanies us in our journey of faith, encouraging readers to be mindful of those before us who have wrestled with an honest faith. As Adam takes the lead on a portion of our trail, his mixture of personal experience, insightful quotes, and practicality illuminates our path when we battle our doubts. As everyone faces the challenges to live in authentic belief, Groza's reminders that faith and doubt can coexist lifts our eyes to Jesus, where we find the answers to our questions. In Christ, doubt will always lose the fight—faith wins! I strongly encourage this book in your daily disciple-making efforts!"

—Christopher Martin, executive director/treasurer, Hawaii Baptist Convention

"*Faith Wins* is a compelling and thought-provoking read for anyone who ever had a crisis of faith or walked through a time of divine uncertainty. It's a journey that allows the reader to not just grow stronger in their faith, but to keep that faith strong even in times of doubt. Prepare to be challenged in the way you view doubt and faith; two things intricately linked. This is a must read!"

—Noe Garcia, senior pastor, North Phoenix Baptist Church

FAITH WINS

Overcoming a Crisis of Belief

ADAM GROZA

NEW HOPE®
PUBLISHERS
Imprint of Iron Stream Media
Birmingham, Alabama

New Hope® Publishers
100 Missionary Ridge
Birmingham, AL 35242
An imprint of Iron Stream Media
NewHopePublishers.com
IronStreamMedia.com

Library of Congress Cataloging-in-Publication Data.

Groza, Adam, 1975- author.
Faith wins : overcoming a crisis of belief / Adam Groza. Birmingham, Alabama:
  New Hope Publishers, 2020.
LCCN 2020019114 (print) | LCCN 2020019115 (ebook) | ISBN 9781563093869 |
  ISBN 9781563093876 (ebook)
Subjects: LCSH: Faith.
Classification: LCC BV4637 .G765 2020 (print) | LCC BV4637 (ebook) |
  DDC 234/.23--dc23
LC record available at https://lccn.loc.gov/2020019114
LC ebook record available at https://lccn.loc.gov/2020019115

ISBN-13: 978-1-56309-386-9
Ebook ISBN: 978-1-56309-387-6

1 2 3 4 5—24 23 22 21 20

To Peter Helms and his parents, Doug and Selah,
who have modeled persevering faith.

With heartfelt acknowledgement of the gentle patience and
gracious support of Holly, Cosette, Charlie, Christian,
and Cate Groza.

My deepest appreciation for the feedback and kind criticism of
Ben Arbour, Jaclyn Brito, Shane Tanigawa, Cameron Schweitzer,
Ben Calcagno, Christine Shen, Deena Carter, Mandie Joachim,
Joe Kim, Kayla Oril, and Andrew Conn.

Contents

Journeying with Christ

My favorite pastime is hiking. The words of John Muir have always resonated with me: "The mountains are calling and I must go." When it comes to hiking, there are two basic options: day hikes and backpacking trips. A day hike is just as it sounds, a trek into the mountains where you leave in the morning and return at night. All you need is one day's provisions, easy to carry in a small backpack.

However, a backpacking trip is much more difficult than a day hike. On a backpacking trip, you need a larger backpack and must carry a heavier load with multiple days of provisions, as well as a tent, sleeping bag, and other essentials. On a backpacking trip you go farther from home, venture deeper into the unknown, and must carry a map or directions so you don't get lost.

Backpacking is a fitting metaphor in many ways for the Christian life. Walking with Christ is a matter of temporary habitation, limited provisions, daily struggle, and directional challenges. In light of this metaphor, consider the words of the Apostle Paul to the church in Corinth:

> For we know that if the tent that is our earthly home is destroyed, we have a building from God, a house not made with hands, eternal in the heavens. For in this tent we groan, longing to put on our heavenly dwelling, if indeed by putting it on we may not be found naked. For while we are still in this tent, we groan, being burdened—not that we would be unclothed, but that we would be further clothed, so that what is mortal may be swallowed up by life. He who has prepared us for this very thing is God, who has given us the Spirit as a guarantee. —2 Corinthians 5:1–5

Paul uses a Greek word for body (*skénos*), which can be translated as tent. If you have ever spent the night in a tent, you know that even a good tent is a poor substitute for your home! A tent is a temporary accommodation fraught with hardship, discomfort, and struggle. In a tent you feel the wind blow, you hear noises in the dark, and only a thin piece of fabric separates you from the wild.

Living in California, there are a number of great places I can hike. Most famous is the Pacific Crest Trail (PCT), which stretches 2,650 miles from the Mexican border in California to the Canadian border in Washington. Thru-hiking the PCT (i.e., going the entire distance in one long continuous hike) requires planning multiple resupply points along the way. Hikers usually buy supplies or pick up boxes of supplies that they (or friends) ship to towns close to the trail. Either way, a long-distance hike necessitates a plan to resupply.

Backpackers subsist mostly on utilitarian foods that are high in calories and lightweight. Eating the same freeze-dried foods day after day gets boring and tedious. For this reason, there are people who show up along the trail and bless hikers with unexpected goodies, something to keep them going and lift their spirits.

Imagine hiking a long distance. Exhausted and famished you come upon a campsite with people handing out free cheeseburgers and cold drinks! For obvious reasons, the kind souls who do this for hikers are called "trail angels," and the food they distribute to weary hikers is called "trail magic."

The Christian life is very much like a long-distance backpacking trip. Every day is a challenge with hardships and rewards. The path is windy, rocky, and contains both beauty and sorrow.

This book is intended to be a bit of trail magic, nourishment for your soul to keep you going on the journey. In her bestselling book *Wild: From Lost to Found on the Pacific Crest Trail*, author Cheryl Strayed says that a trail offers two options. You can either go back in the direction you came from or go forward in the direction you intended to go.

I hope this book serves as a resupply point for your journey forward.

Chapter 1

Don't Panic: Go Forward

At some point, everybody goes through a crisis of faith. You may even be in one right now. How does it feel to go through a crisis of faith? It feels like the room is spinning and the ground is shifting: Like a sucker punch to the soul.

You know how that feels. At some point growing up, most of us wander from our parents and realize in a moment of panic that we are lost. It happened to me once in a department store. One moment I was holding my mother's hand, and then the next moment I was lost in a forest of clothes racks, disoriented, and feeling totally alone. A crisis of faith feels like being suddenly lost and without bearing.

That is how doubt *feels*. But what is a crisis of faith? How do you define it to someone who has never endured the existential crisis of sudden unbelief? I define a crisis of faith as a time of spiritual doubt, anxiety, or despair. In such a time, doubt *exceeds* faith.

It seems odd to talk about faith and doubt together. It should be faith or doubt, not faith and doubt. We tend to think of faith and doubt like oil and water, toasters and bathtubs, or Apple and Microsoft. But they are like Chang and Eng Bunker. They are where we got the term "Siamese twins," now known as conjoined twins. Chang and Eng went from indentured servitude to international stardom in the nineteenth century, all while being awkwardly and painfully connected at the side. Somehow they managed to acquire success, wealth, spouses, and between them have twenty-one children.

Faith and doubt exist awkwardly and painfully in the hearts of Christians. We are both the person we are becoming and the person we used to be: the new man and the old man, side by side, make their way through life. Somehow, despite the spectacle of our messy journey, God accomplishes more than we could ever imagine.

Faith Like a Dimmer Switch

One common myth we must dispel from the outset is that faith is the absence of doubt. According to this myth, you either believe or you don't. This view of faith is much like a light switch where faith is either on or off.

In regard to saving faith—the faith that justifies—the light switch analogy works. Romans 5:1 says, "Therefore, since we have been justified by faith, we have peace with God through our Lord Jesus Christ." Saving faith is described as a gift (Ephesians 2:8–10). Whoever believes in Jesus will not perish but has eternal life (John 3:16).

But the gift of faith, once possessed, is more like a dimmer switch. A dimmer switch is not so much on or off as it is bright or dim. If you have a room with a dimmer switch, the light can be barely visible but still on, or it can be radiant. There are varying degrees to which the light and the darkness inhabit the same space. Jesus is the only man of whom it could be said, "In him is no darkness at all" (1 John 1:5).

The image of faith like a dimmer switch is the one pictured in the Bible. A man comes to Jesus in Mark 9 with a son who is possessed by a demon. The demon is trying to destroy the boy by throwing him into fire or water (v. 22).

Imagine for a moment this father's sense of desperation. Imagine a demon possessing your child and trying to destroy him. The good news is that Jesus is fully God and has power over life and death. He has mercy on the father and his son, casting out the demon and commanding it never to return. Jesus is flexing His power over sin and death. It's a taste of his coming victory on the Cross.

Jesus says to the father, "All things are possible for one who believes" (v. 23). This isn't a blank check guaranteeing health and wealth in this life. John Calvin, in his commentary on Mark 9, points out that Jesus is promising that by faith in Him we access all the blessings of God, but we do not experience all His blessings until we are glorified in His presence. Until that day Christians struggle with doubt, suffering, and all kinds of evil. Remember the story of the prodigal son? It is dangerous and faithless to demand an early inheritance.

The father of the demon-possessed child hears the command to believe and responds by crying out to Jesus in tears, "I believe; help my unbelief!" (v. 24). Here is biblical faith. It is a mixture of faith and unbelief varying by degree depending on the day, the hour, and sometimes even the minute. Biblical faith is not the absence of doubt but the perseverance of belief over doubt. In other words, faith wins.

Doubt, in itself, is not a good thing. Unbelief is not a virtue. Christians should beware any teacher or movement that glorifies unbelief. Jesus tells Thomas, "Stop doubting and believe" (John 20:27 NIV). James says we must ask in faith without doubting, for "the one who doubts is like a wave of the sea that is driven and tossed by the wind" (James 1:6). Doubt and unbelief are sins and the root of all sin (Romans 14:23).

However, until we are made perfect with Jesus in heaven, we possess faith like a dimmer switch. We can (and should) pray the prayer of the unnamed father in Mark's story: *I believe; help my unbelief.* Knowledge and faith coexist with uncertainty and doubt.

In another biblical account, the disciples were on a boat with Jesus when a sudden storm made them fear for their lives. Jesus was asleep, a picture of calm trust and confidence. The disciples woke Him up, Jesus rebuked the waves as only God can do, and then He rebuked His disciples: "You of little faith" (Matthew 8:26).

Did you notice what Jesus says about faith? Faith can be little; it can be dim. At the same time, faith can grow. Peter exhorts believers to "grow in the grace and knowledge of our Lord and Savior Jesus Christ" (2 Peter 3:18). Paul says Christians should "grow up in every way" (Ephesians 4:15) and become mature (1 Corinthians 14:20).

There are two fundamental questions about faith. First, do you have saving faith? This question is not settled by you alone. It is resolved in the context of a local church, starting with your profession of faith then including your public declaration of faith and repentance through baptism and at the Lord's Supper, reflecting an ongoing desire to follow Jesus and to be in community with His people. The second question builds upon the first: If you have saving faith, how is your faith? Is it weak or strong? Is it bright or dim? Possessing faith is not the same thing as growing in faith and being strong in faith.

The Confession of Unbelief

From beginning to end, faith is a gift from God (Ephesians 2:8–10). The gift of faith is experienced in our fallen state: sin ruins everything. "Help my unbelief" is not a commendation of doubt but a cry for sanctification. It is a confession.

Have you ever heard someone confess the sin of unbelief or doubt? Or even admit to the struggle? If the biblical picture of faith is one of flux, why the impulse to pretend that faith is static and immovable? We tend to act as though our faith were immovable, like God.

Perhaps there are two reasons it is hard to confess to unbelief. Primarily we have wrongly been taught that faith is the absence of doubt. C. S. Lewis writes in *The Screwtape Letters* that courage is the testing point of all the virtues. Courage puts virtue into action. Without courage, love is a banging gong or a crashing symbol (1 Corinthians 13:1). Without courage, virtue is impotent.

A crisis of faith is the testing point of belief. We find out what kind of stuff our faith is made of. A crisis of faith turns us inside out; it shows us what is inside. A crisis of faith is good in the end but painful in the moment.

Doubt is the feeling or the sense that something you previously believed to be true might not be true after all. Something you thought you knew, perhaps you do not know. It is a period of spiritual vertigo. The sense that things are out of control.

When Christians struggle with doubt, they should confess doubt, and when they do, they should receive mercy. Jude says as much: "Have mercy on those who doubt" (Jude 1:22). Jude was someone who knew about doubt.

Jude is a small book in the New Testament written by Jesus's brother, Jude. Contrary to the teaching of the Roman Catholic Church, Mary and Joseph went on to have children after Jesus was born. Jesus had brothers! Just like Joseph's brothers rejected Joseph, John reports that Jesus's brothers didn't believe in Him (John 7:5). Not one of them is mentioned as being a disciple prior to His crucifixion.

Jesus didn't always have the support of His family. However Luke reports that after the crucifixion the disciples were all with "one accord were devoting themselves to prayer, together with the women and Mary the mother of Jesus, and his brothers" (Acts 1:14).

Jude came to faith but understood the ongoing battle of unbelief and the need for mercy. The battle of the mind demands that thoughts be taken captive to the obedience of Christ (2 Corinthians 10:5). There would be no need for such an exhortation if the mind were not a battlefield where faith waged daily war against unbelief. No wonder Scripture is called the "sword of the Spirit" (Ephesians 6:17).

A healthy Christian environment is one in which the war of faith and doubt is understood, where Christians can confess their unbelief and find mercy in the context of the local church. This is what it looks like to practice honest faith.

Pretend Faith vs. Honest Faith

Some time ago, my wife and I were at a family dinner when one relative shared his experience about growing up in a "Christian home." He wasn't able to ask questions about God, the Bible, or what the church believed. In his home, faith was just doing what you were told, saying the right things, and never asking why. Faith meant pretending as though he didn't have doubts or questions.

Someone can be saved by faith and yet operate in an unbiblical manner with their faith. This is the difference between pretend faith and honest faith. Pretend faith follows the dictum of pyramid schemes: fake it till you make it.

Pretend faith acts confidently to hide doubt. It poses and pretends to understand even when things don't make sense. In the song "Aaron Burr, Sir," on the hit Broadway musical soundtrack *Hamilton*, Aaron Burr advises Alexander Hamilton to do more smiling and less talking! Such advice epitomizes the hypocrisy of pretend faith.

In Christian community, pretend faith hides questions, smiles through pain, buries sin, ignores challenging doctrines, and glosses over disagreement. Pretend faith would never confront Peter like Paul did in Galatians 2. Pretend faith would never have written Gospel accounts in which Peter denies Jesus, Thomas doubts, and the disciples routinely display a lack of faith. Pretend faith is inauthentic, disingenuous, and saccharine.

In their book *The Subtle Power of Spiritual Abuse*, authors David Johnson and Jeff VanVonderen outline how systems of abuse are built on the misguided notion that faith never questions, confronts, or pushes back. Pretend faith traffics in manipulation, control, and shame. Abusive systems are, in essence, built upon pretend faith.

God is not abusive. His commands come with reasons. He tells Adam and Eve to stay away from certain fruit "for in the day that you eat of it you shall surely die" (Genesis 2:17). Children are to obey their parents "so that you may live long in the land" (Exodus 20:12 NIV). God's commands are reasonable, and His instructions usually come with explanation. God graciously anticipates our questions. Why not eat the fruit? Why should I obey my parents? When Christians stifle charitable inquiry—what Anselm of Canterbury called *fides quaerens intellectum* (faith seeking understanding)—they are not acting like their Heavenly Father.

The Bible paints a radically different picture of honest faith. In contrast to pretend faith, honest faith asks questions, admits pain, confesses sin, dives deep, and works through disagreement. Honest faith admits struggle as Paul does in Romans 7, confronts division as Paul does in 1 Corinthians 1, and even admits publicly to moments of disagreement among leaders as between Paul and John Mark in Acts 15.

Honest faith doesn't hide failure. The disciples were unable to cast out demons in Matthew 17, and *they wrote about it*! The Sons of Sceva got beat up by demons in Acts 19, and Luke told us the story. Whole letters of the Bible such as 1 Corinthians and Galatians outline failure in the church. Why is the Bible so candid? The purpose in telling stories of failure is to grow and promote genuine spiritual health. Honest faith doesn't dwell on failure, divisions, and doubts, but it uses these moments to bring clarity and maturity to the church.

The Paradox of Honest Faith

Honest faith is a kind of paradox. In his book *The Paradoxes of Mr. Pond*,

G. K. Chesterton says that a paradox is the truth stranding on its head begging for attention. It would appear that honest faith would discourage belief, but it actually strengthens belief.

Consider a father who comes to his children in humility and contrition, saying, "Please forgive me; I was wrong about what I said. It was untrue, thoughtless, and it didn't communicate God's grace and love." Provided this man makes a serious effort to correct his ways, his humility and contrition will result in respect and admiration. His children will see what it looks like for a man to possess honest faith.

The Bible is filled with paradoxes. We are made strong in our weakness (Hebrews 11:34). The first shall be last (Matthew 20:16). Lose your life, and you will find it (Matthew 10:39). The wisdom of God is foolishness (1 Corinthians 1:18). Salvation is by faith alone (not by works) but saving faith works itself out in obedience (Ephesians 2:8–10 and James 2:20).

Think for a moment about the paradox of salvation. In the wilderness of Sinai, the Israelites tested God and were cursed with fiery serpents (Numbers 21). God had mercy on Israel and instructed Moses to make a bronze serpent, put it on a stick, and hold it up. Whoever looked upon the image of the cursed thing would be saved. Imagine, looking upon the curse in order to be saved!

In perhaps the most famous passage in the Bible, John starts a sentence by saying "For God so loved the world" (John 3:16). You know the verse, but you may have missed what John is saying. We tend to read the phrase "so loved" to indicate emphasis, as in "I love you *so* much." In reality, John is making a reference. You could translate it this way: *This* is how God loved the world.

John is referring to the preceding verses: "And as Moses lifted up the serpent in the wilderness, so must the Son of Man be lifted up, that whoever believes in him may have eternal life" (v. 15). John is referring to the scene in the Book of Numbers where Israel's only hope is to look upon the cursed thing in order to be saved.

So when John says, "For God so loved the world, that he gave his only Son, that whoever believes in him should not perish but have eternal life" (v. 16), he is saying everyone is self-infected with sin and Jesus became the curse so that if we look to Him and believe, we will be saved. Paul says, "Christ redeemed us from the curse of the law by becoming a curse for us—for it is written, 'Cursed is everyone who is hanged on a tree'" (Galatians 3:13).

These paradoxes are initially disorienting. Jesus became sin so we would become righteous (2 Corinthians 5:21). The cure becomes the curse so those cursed can become cured.

So what's the point of a paradox? It draws attention to truth. Biblical paradoxes highlight the truth of Scripture, not undermine it. Paradoxes in the Bible are not illogical.

Think of biblical paradoxes as evidence that God's ways are not our ways and that His thoughts are higher than ours (Isaiah 55:8–9). As scientist Johannes Kepler would say, we are merely thinking God's thoughts after Him. A paradox gets our attention, makes us think, challenges our laziness, and rewards us with a deeper understanding of the gospel.

In regard to faith, the paradox is that confessing doubt is a sign of faith, not a sign that you lack faith. In 1855 Charles Spurgeon delivered a sermon titled "Desire of the Soul in Spiritual Darkness." His text was Isaiah 26:9, which says, "My soul yearns for you in the night." In the sermon, Spurgeon said:

> I think, when a man says, "I never doubt," it is quite time for us to doubt him, it is quite time for us to begin to say, "Ah, poor soul, I am afraid you are not on the road at all, for if you were, you would see so many things in yourself, and so much glory in Christ more than you deserve, that you would be so much ashamed of yourself, as even to say, 'It is too good to be true.'"

A person who says they never doubt doesn't seem to possess honest faith. You cannot help seeing more of your sin when you see more of Christ. The result is a lifelong cycle of spiritual growth and doubt. Experiencing that cycle, according to Spurgeon, is an indication that you are "on the road" of honest (i.e., genuine or saving) faith.

The paradox of honest faith is that submission to God brings true freedom, even though we fear it will restrict our freedom. Confession seems like it would make us look weak, but it displays God's strength in us. Asking questions and seeking clarity does not imply a lack of faith but a faith trying to grow and mature.

Biblical Heroes in the Hall of Faith

Hebrews 11 is often called the Hall of Faith. Biblical characters are listed and commended for their faith in Jesus, even though none of them had the privilege of knowing His name. On the list are the usual suspects—Abraham, Moses, Rahab, and David.

The Bible holds up these individuals. They are "commended through their faith" (v. 39). They are the examples of what it looks like to have saving faith. And yet the Bible reveals in each of their stories times of doubt, uncertainty, and faithlessness. Each of them went through what we would call a crisis of faith.

Abraham doubts that God will provide him a son, and so he goes his own way and has a child with Hagar, who is not his wife. Moses doubted and gave a list of excuses for not wanting to be God's spokesman (Exodus 3:11, 13; 4:1, 10–13). David doubted and wrote songs about it: "How long, O LORD? Will you forget me forever?" (Psalm 13:1). Rahab and Abraham lied.

This forces us to redefine what it means to be a hero of the faith. A hero of the faith is not someone who never doubts but rather someone who trusts God through their doubt and uncertainty. Our doubt and uncertainty shine a spotlight on God's unflinching faithfulness: He is the real hero of the story. Honest faith accomplishes what John the Baptist prayed: I must decrease, and He must increase (John 3:30).

Doubt Is Normal

The first lesson that these heroes of faith teach us is that doubt is normal. A person who doubts should not assume they are not saved, that something is wrong, or that they must have failed. Sin affects every aspect of life, including our thought life. Paul says, "For although they knew God, they did not honor him as God or give thanks to him, but they became futile in their thinking, and their foolish hearts were darkened" (Romans 1:21).

Because sin affects our thinking, the life of faith is a constant battle between belief and doubt. For this reason, Paul commands Christians to be transformed by the renewing of your mind (Romans 12:2). Doubt is not good, but it is normal.

Matthew 28 is famous, primarily because it contains what is often referred to as the Great Commission. It occurred after Jesus rose from the dead and gathered his eleven remaining disciples on a mountain:

> Now the eleven disciples went to Galilee, to the mountain to which Jesus had directed them. And when they saw him they worshiped him, but some doubted. And Jesus came and said to them, "All authority in heaven and on earth has been given to me. Go therefore and make disciples of all nations, baptizing them in the name of the Father and of the Son and of the Holy Spirit, teaching them to observe all that I have commanded you. And behold, I am with you always, to the end of the age.
> —Matthew 28:16–20

We move so quickly to the Great Commission that we miss an astounding fact about this last earthly meeting between Jesus and His disciples: It says some doubted. Who doubted? It doesn't say. It only says "some," meaning more than one. There were only eleven disciples present, so at the very least there were two doubting, which means at least 18 percent of the disciples doubted while Jesus stood with them!

These men had walked with Jesus, been taught by Jesus, seen the miracles, witnessed the crucifixion and resurrection, and Jesus had opened their minds to understand the Scriptures.

And yet some doubted.

At every stage the disciples experienced doubt. Why then are you surprised to find yourself struggling with doubt? Maybe you have been a Christian for a long time, but until you are made perfect with Christ, you will always battle some level of unbelief. In fact, the more you learn about God, the more you understand His holiness and your sinfulness, the more likely you are to struggle with doubt.

This is the paradox of honest faith. Doubt should not surprise us. We should ask good questions, wrestle with the meaning and application of scriptural passages, and struggle to make sense of our faith; these are signs of healthy spiritual growth. All growth comes with growing pains, and spiritual growth is no different. Doubt is often a sign of spiritual growth.

Faith Over Doubt

Dr. Martyn Lloyd-Jones was a twentieth-century Welsh theologian, pastor, and medical doctor. He wrote a book on spiritual depression called *Spiritual Depression: Its Causes and Cures*, in which he says the following:

> Faith is a refusal to panic. Do you like that sort of definition of faith? Does that seem to be too earthly and not sufficiently spiritual? It is of the very essence of faith. Faith is a refusal to panic, come what may. Browning, I think, had that idea when he defined faith like this: "With me, faith means perpetual unbelief kept quiet, like the snake 'neath Michael's foot." Here is Michael and there is the snake beneath his foot, and he just keeps it quiet under the pressure of his foot. Faith is unbelief kept quiet, kept down. That is what these men did not do, they allowed this situation to grip them, they became panicky. Faith, however, is a refusal to allow that. It says: "I am not going to be controlled by these circumstances—I am in control." So you take charge of yourself, and pull yourself up, you control yourself. You do not let yourself go, you assert yourself.

Lloyd-Jones sees biblical faith and unbelief as coexisting in the life of a believer. What we learn to do as mature Christians is assert faith over doubt, to control ourselves by not letting doubt overwhelm faith. This is a picture of active faith, not passive faith.

Doubt can make us feel out of control. The panic of unbelief is the sensation of losing your bearings, of feeling disoriented. Asserting faith over doubt means preaching to yourself rather than listening to yourself. It is the active exercise of the will to believe. As the man prays to Jesus, "Help my unbelief." The man wanted to believe more and doubt less. He refused to surrender his faith to his doubts.

The nineteenth-century German philosopher Friedrich Nietzsche is famous for declaring that "God is dead" in his book *The Gay Science* (an English title which is now a misleading translation of the German title *Die fröhliche Wissenschaft*, which could be more accurately translated as *the joyful or happy science*). With God out of the way, Nietzsche believed humankind was capable of making our own rules and asserting our will to power.

Nietzsche is a tragic figure in many ways. Sadly, he seemed to think God stood in the way of the will. Either God exists and the will is passive, or there is no God, and the will is set free to be active. In other words, Nietzsche's God is a domesticating cosmic wet blanket who wants to subdue our will. Or as Karl Marx puts it, God is a sort of divine opiate for the masses.

The Bible does teach that we must submit our will to God's will. Jesus prayed and teaches us to pray, "Your will be done" (Matthew 6:10). Jesus (God the Son) submitted His will to God the Father as evidence of His sinless humanity.

Our sinful and fallen wills are enemies of God and must be subdued by force of the Spirit through conversion. At the moment of salvation, the Spirit moves in and takes over. Even after we are saved, however, we continue to struggle against the sinful desires of the flesh that are contrary to the Spirit (Romans 7:13–25). We must submit to God by killing sinful desires (i.e., desires of the flesh) in order to awaken new desires from the Spirit and then live according to those new desires.

Submission is a willful act. When God saves a person, their will is activated by the Spirit to engage in faithful obedience. This includes submission. The ethos of "let go and let God" is more Eastern mysticism than it is biblical. Nietzsche was wrong to think God stood opposed to the human will. Through a relationship with God, the will is set free to flourish. When a human flourishes, we experience what ancient Greek philosophers called *Eudaimonia*.

Jude 1:3 says we are to "contend for the faith that was once for all delivered to the saints." The word *contend* in the Greek (*epagónizomai*) is a compound word used only once in the New Testament. Part of the word comes from the Greek word (*agón*) from which we get our word for agony. To contend means something like an intense and focused struggle.

We are to struggle for our faith. This is entirely a picture of the active will. Like Jacob wrestled with the angel, Christians engage in daily spiritual battle for faith over doubt. The struggle is intense and, at times, spiritually agonizing. No wonder David cried out, "How long, O Lord?"

Of course, David's faith is active. He preaches to himself, declaring, "My heart shall rejoice in your salvation" (Psalm 13:5). David contends for his own faith. He commands his soul to praise God, saying, "Bless the Lord, O my soul!" (Psalm 104:1). Passive faith waits for the moment to be right and the stars to align. Passive faith insists on certain aesthetics and emotions; like Goldilocks, things must be just right.

But biblical faith is rugged and determined. Biblical faith asserts belief over doubt, like Paul singing hymns in the prison (Acts 16:25), Jesus praying in the Garden (Matthew 26:36–56), or Stephen looking to Jesus while being stoned to death (Acts 7:55).

Active faith is warfare. It is determined to advance. As missionary David Livingstone said while looking out over the morning fires on the African continent: "I will go anywhere, provided it be forward."

Oscar Wilde said that belief is dull, and doubt is intensely engrossing. Wilde may be right if he is speaking about what we have called pretend faith, which is passive. On the other hand, he is wrong about biblical faith, or what we have called honest faith, which is active and adventurous. Faith grows and aches like a muscle being worked out.

God never panics. Christian faith is anchored in God. He is never surprised or overwhelmed.

The Nausea of Crippling Unbelief

Doubt can be paralyzing and absorbing. It is like quicksand; the more you struggle, the more you sink. In a true crisis of faith, a believer (someone with true saving faith) stares down the emptiness of the possibility of life without God—the ultimate gut check.

In John 6 Jesus teaches on a difficult subject—eating His body and drinking His blood. Of course, it is a metaphor for consuming Jesus by faith and receiving Him as the sacrificial lamb as the sacrificial lamb, just as the Israelites ate the spotless lamb on the night of Passover. Jesus is identifying Himself as the spotless Lamb of God.

Still, it says most of the people left. They simply did not have eyes to see or ears to hear. Jesus turned to His disciples and said, "What about you guys? Are you going to leave too?" Of course Jesus knew they would not leave; I read this as more of a challenge than a question.

Peter responds (of course he does) with a surprisingly insightful counter-question, which I imagine made Jesus smile: "To whom shall we go? You have the words of eternal life" (v. 68). In moments of doubt, it is helpful to seriously consider the alternatives. If you abandon Jesus, where will you go? Who else will impart meaning to life? No other system of belief is more convincing, more historical, more cohesive, and more fulfilling.

At some point in your youth you probably flirted with the idea of running away. I remember having that impulse on several occasions, and one or two times I even packed a backpack with my things and walked out the door defiantly saying, "I'm outta here!"

And then I walked around the block. Maybe went to Circle K and got a soda. Stopped by a friend's house until his parents told me to go home. You see, leaving is easy. Finding somewhere else to go—somewhere better—is hard. In the case of Christianity, it is impossible.

In a crisis of faith, we are tempted to leave the faith, run for the door, and find another house with a warmer fire and a softer bed. The grass is never greener. To whom else shall we go? Peter has it right.

Still, the exercise of mentally running away from the faith can be helpful. What if there is no God? Play that scenario out and see if you like the alternative. To whom else will you go?

Someone who did just that is French philosopher Jean-Paul Sartre in his philosophical novel *Nausea*. Its protagonist is named Roquentin, who embodies a person living as though God doesn't exist. With no God, Roquentin discovers that there is no moral order, purpose, or justice. In other words, without God, life is absurd and meaningless.

In some sense, Roquentin is free. And yet, as he says, "I am free; there is absolutely no more reason for living." Freedom is not absolute. It is good in relation to God, but not in itself. Freedom in itself is a crippling and overwhelming abstraction. It ultimately cancels itself out, because ultimate freedom is, as Roquentin observes, a kind of prison: the prison of self.

Sociologists talk about the paradox of choice. As it turns out, the more choices we have, the less happiness we experience. You have likely stood in a supermarket aisle staring at a wall of cereal, totally overwhelmed by the choices, only to walk away having chosen nothing. Or you may have gone to a restaurant for lunch only to find out the restaurant you chose has an unusually large menu. You walk in hungry, only to stare at the pages of choices without a clue what you want to eat. Here you are, hungry, but with more choices than you can imagine, crippled by indecision.

Sartre says that feeling of indecision, of the paralysis that comes from the absolute freedom to choose, induces a sense of nausea. What you thought you wanted (Cereal! Lunch!) is now repulsive. These things represent freedom, but freedom in itself (apart from God) presents too many choices and no reason to choose.

Unbelief can feel like nausea. Like your soul is dizzy. The waves of unbelief that James talks about feel like seasickness (James 1:6).

Certain experiences trigger the nausea of unbelief. Fall to certain temptations, and you will wake up with the hangover of doubt and spiritual anxiety. Unexpected tragedy has the physical and spiritual effect of making you sick to your stomach. A financial setback can feel like stomach flu.

For many of us, college was a minefield of doubt—bad relationships, newfound freedoms, intellectual challenges, exposure to religious hypocrisy. It's a recipe for a crisis of faith.

Like an addict learns what triggers their cravings, a Christian learns what triggers unbelief. We learn to identify the monster and call it by name: unbelief.

Why do these situations trigger unbelief? What is the anatomy of unbelief?

Doubt is never merely intellectual. Doubt is always personal. When we doubt we allow ourselves to question God. We are saying, "I don't know if I can trust You, God."

And it's downhill from there. God gives meaning, stability, and structure to life. His Word is our compass. It is our guide. Questioning Him induces the vertigo of unbelief. "Where are You, God? Are You even there? Why didn't You provide? Why didn't You protect? You have good reasons, but they are unknown to me."

"Help my unbelief." That's about the only kind of prayer we can utter in moments of spiritual disorientation. "How long, O Lord?"

Yet God's children do not stay in the valley of the shadow of death. They move through it to green pastures. In the Bible, God shows us how to move from point A to point B.

Overcoming doubt requires the will to believe. It requires active and honest faith. But more than that, it requires a strategy learned from the Bible. Ironically, we learn how to overcome doubt from the very heroes of faith who persevered through doubt.

Getting Through a Crisis of Faith

What is your strategy for making it through a crisis of faith? It is best to have one before devastation strikes. Before being in the hospital room and hearing the dreaded news. Before the next market crash. Before you experience betrayal.

The rest of this book is dedicated to that purpose. The following chapters develop a strategy for overcoming doubt by looking at how the doubting heroes of the faith made it to the end with their faith intact. We will see examples of honest faith struggling to grow and mature.

One thing is sure: In a crisis of faith, there is no silver bullet. The strategy we develop will involve varied lines of attack. These tactics learned from Scripture will have the cumulative effect of reviving faith, even faith that appears terminal. If there is faith, however small, however dim, then there is hope. God is in the business of fanning sparks into flames.

God bolsters our faith in certain ways. We cannot manipulate God, but His ways are dependable. There is a path of grace, and we can at the very least put ourselves in the places and postures where doubt weakens and faith grows stronger.

Do not miss the point: God intends to make us stronger. He does not want to coddle spiritual fragility. In the book *Antifragile: Things That Gain From Disorder*, author Nassim Nicholas Taleb says, "Antifragility is beyond resilience or robustness. The resilient resists shocks and stays the same; the antifragile gets better."

A crisis of faith is ultimately a means of growing stronger in faith. Christians possess the Spirit of God and are therefore antifragile, growing through hardships:

> We are afflicted in every way, but not crushed; perplexed, but not driven to despair; persecuted, but not forsaken; struck down, but not destroyed; always carrying in the body the death of Jesus, so that the life of Jesus may also be manifested in our bodies. For we who live are always being given over to death for

Jesus' sake, so that the life of Jesus also may be manifested in
our mortal flesh. . . . So we do not lose heart. Though our outer
self is wasting away, our inner self is being renewed day by day.
—2 Corinthians 4:8–11, 16

In *Antifragile*, Taleb references the ancient Greek myth of Hydra, a
snake-like creature with many heads. Cut off one of its heads, and two
would grow back. Hydra had no need to fear danger because it only
made it stronger. Hydra represents antifragility and, for Christians, the
bounce-back factor of spiritual vitality made possible by God's Spirit.

If you are in a crisis of faith, it will take time to work through
this book and learn the strategy and put the steps into practice. In the
meantime, commit to the following to give yourself a fighting chance:

1. Pray: It doesn't matter whether or not you feel like praying.
   Pray anyway. You can pick up your Bible right now, turn to
   Lamentations 3:1, and start praying the brokenhearted words
   of Jeremiah, "I am the man who has seen affliction." Keep reading, and keep praying.

2. Go to Church: This may seem counterintuitive. Some may
   think church is a place for the faithful, not the doubtful, and
   so in times of doubt, they avoid church. But church is the
   perfect place in times of doubt. At a healthy, Bible-believing
   church you will hear Scripture taught and believers worship.
   God speaks as His Word is read, proclaimed, and sung. Join
   in the reading and in the singing, and in doing the things that
   believers do, you might find yourself believing.

3. Keep Seeking: Listen to the words of seventeenth-century philosopher Blaise Pascal from his book *Thoughts*: "Surely then
   it is a great evil thus to be in doubt, but it is at least an indispensable duty to seek when we are in such doubt; and thus the
   doubter who does not seek is altogether completely unhappy
   and completely wrong." Worse than doubt is resigning yourself
   to doubt. Go down fighting. At least in the fight there is the
   hope of the possibility of victory. Resigning yourself to defeat
   will only intensify the experience of doubt.

4. Do Not Be Impulsive: A life of faith should not be undone or
   overshadowed by a crisis of faith. Seek counseling. Get help.

But do not repudiate something publicly just because today you find it difficult to believe. Be honest about your doubt with trusted friends, your church small group, or a Christian counselor. But venting your crisis of faith in public (think social media) is likely to bring more heat than light.

5. Take a Breath and Remember Some of Your Past Spiritual Victories: The experience of failure often lasts longer than your experience of success. Seasons of doubt triggered by personal failure seem to last a long time because they do. Turns out, most of us see the glass half empty.

But God has wired us with an amazing capability for digging ourselves out of a spiritual funk. There is something called synthetic happiness, and it is our ability to generate happiness through thought. We don't need to have met that special someone to be happy; we can get happy just by thinking about *what it would be like* to meet that person. People watch cooking shows because while we may be on a diet, at least we can watch someone else bake (and eat) cookies and remember a time when we were able to enjoy our favorite desserts. Whether we eat the cookies, smell the cookies, or even just imagine the cookies, we experience a newfound sense of joy.

So in times of doubt initiated by the defeat of sin, after you have confessed and while you are repenting, spend some time remembering a spiritual victory. Remember how good it felt to obey. This will not only activate joy; it will help set a course for future obedience.

On several occasions, God told Israel to make a monument to remember past victories. He had them set up stones after crossing the Jordan (Joshua 4:1–7). He had them carry around artifacts of His faithfulness to remind them of His presence (Hebrews 9:4). These monuments and artifacts had the dual effect of both encouraging faithfulness and reminding Israel to keep looking to God.

Former United States Navy SEAL and professional endurance athlete David Goggins has talked about how he gets through grueling ultra-races that exceed one hundred miles of running, some of them in the most inhospitable conditions. He has a strategy he calls "going to the cookie jar," a metaphor he uses in his book *Can't Hurt Me* for giving yourself a mental treat. When Goggins is running and feeling tired, he forces himself to think about previous victories. Going to the cookie jar has the cognitive effect of producing synthetic happiness: He feels the residual effects of past victory. The physical effect is a release of endorphins and an energy boost to keep him going in the race.

Hope in Seasons of Doubt

If faith is like an endurance race, and if doubt is part of the pain that comes with running the race, then the ultimate consolation is not in good memories alone but in knowing there is a finish line. Doubt has an expiration date. Union with Christ after death is the end of doubt and the perfection of faith.

Despair, when it is rational, is a combination of not liking the way things are and feeling as though they will never change. Remove either of these things, and you eliminate despair. Circumstances that lead us to doubt faith are often outside our control. We don't like going through trauma, betrayal, illness, or financial hardships.

In some cases, God gives us the grace to make changes in life through wise decisions, good planning, and smart execution. An unhappy marriage that results in a crisis of faith may be remedied by biblical counseling and intentional personal changes. A financial hardship that results from chronic overspending is likely to test your faith, but self-control and disciplined budgeting brings light at the end of the tunnel.

In other cases, struggle with doubt can seem hopeless because either your situation doesn't change despite your best efforts or your situation is made difficult by factors outside your control (i.e., sickness). In either case, you confront the reality that life is hard. As it says in Job, life is "few of days and full of trouble" (Job 14:1).

In Greek mythology, King Sisyphus was condemned to push a rock up a mountain. Once at the top, the rock rolled back down, and he had to roll it back up, over and over again. We despair when life is thankless, tedious, and monotonous.

Paul experienced more than his share of hardship and doubt. What was his secret? He says, "I press on toward the goal for the prize of the upward call of God in Christ Jesus" (Philippians 3:14). In other words, I am going somewhere to be with someone. God is the reward. We get to be with God. That coming reality gives faith the ability to endure to the end and cross the finish line.

Heaven has fallen on hard times. It seems there is a reluctance to talk about heaven. Several things may account for this trend. We may be overcorrecting for the thief-in-the-night view of the end times that led some Christians to focus on heaven so much they fail to engage their communities for Christ or live in fear of being "left behind." Others may fear that talking about heaven will distract us from the work of social engagement and make us too heavenly minded to be of any earthly good.

Martin Luther observed that Christians tend to be like drunk men on horses—we either fall off one side of the other. We owe it to ourselves to strike a biblical balance between putting our hands to the plow and taking a break to consider the harvest.

On one hand, there is work to be done to fight for faith, to run the race, to take responsibility, and battle unbelief. At the same time there is rest in Christ and a coming day of union with Christ when faith becomes sight and all doubt ceases. We look forward to that day in a way that energizes effort and activates gospel engagement.

A strategy for dealing with doubt—such as this book offers—requires a view of the finish line. Living the life of faith is like committing to reading a long and somewhat difficult book. The story is good, but it takes persistence. Especially because the ending is worth the effort.

And so you keep reading, keep trusting, and keep running. It won't always be hard. There is a finish line and a reward ceremony. Best of all, there is a person waiting to welcome you after a long and difficult journey.

In his classic book *Lectures to My Students*, nineteenth-century British pastor Charles Spurgeon wrote on the need for personal progress, saying, "Every man should be made the most of, and nerved to his highest point of strength." Spurgeon's point is that no one is static in the faith; every Christian (especially a Christian leader) is either going forward or backward in the faith. He encourages the reader to go forward:

I give you the motto, "Go forward." *Go forward* in personal attainments, *forward* in gifts and in grace, *forward* in fitness for the work, and *forward* in conformity to the image of Jesus.

It is true that doubt and faith coexist, but saving faith wins in the end. Be honest about your doubt and take charge of your faith. Don't panic; keep moving *forward*.

Chapter 2

John the Baptist: Are You the Messiah?

*E*nglish poet Thomas Gray penned the infamous phrase "ignorance is bliss." It comes from Gray's poem *Ode on a Distant Prospect of Eton College,* in which he writes from the perspective of an adult looking back on his youth. These words are timeless because the sentiment is universal: With knowledge and experience comes pain and suffering. Or, as Westley says in the classic movie *The Princess Bride*, "Life is pain."

Jesus says in this life you will have suffering (John 16:33). The more life that you live, the more pain and suffering you will endure. We said in chapter one that indwelling sin, suffering, and other personal traumas lead to doubt. Add to this list daily experiences of living in a fallen world where natural evil abounds.

Natural evil is a term philosophers and theologians use for the kind of suffering that comes from the natural world, such as cancer and earthquakes. Natural evil leads to doubt because our experience of suffering takes place against the backdrop of God's sovereignty and perfect knowledge of all events past, present, and future.

God is never surprised. He knows everything (1 John 3:20). He knows what has happened, what could happen, and what will happen. God is not only omniscient (i.e., perfect in knowledge), but he is also omnipotent (i.e., perfect in power). God knows what will happen and can allow or prevent anything from happening according to His will.

Given what God tells us about Himself, when bad things happen, Christians struggle to reconcile God's perfect goodness with His perfect knowledge and power. This kind of explanation for the reason-ableness of faith, given the amount and intensity of suffering, is called a theodicy, a word that comes from the Greek words for God (*Theos*) and justice (*dikē*).

Why do bad things happen? Of course, no one can explain all the reasons God allows what He allows. But just because we cannot explain everything does not mean we cannot explain anything. We know God is good. We know God is in control. We know God has good reasons for doing and allowing all that takes place. We even know He uses bad things for His glory and our good (Romans 8:28).

This knowledge brings peace, but it doesn't dull pain. On the Cross, Jesus knew the joy that was before Him, but He suffered the full wrath of God and the injustice of humankind in the moment (Hebrews 12:2). Good theology will keep you in the faith, but it will not keep you from suffering.

An Unexpected Source of Doubt

At some point God's Word (the Bible) is going to make you mad. It will say something you do not like. Some story will not make sense. God will say something you wish He had not.

During my freshman year of college at Northern Arizona University, I was excited to explore my newfound faith in Jesus. I found a church a short walk from my dorm since I did not have a car. Walking into that small church and sitting in the back pew, two things happened that forever changed my life.

First the pastor said, "Open your Bible," and proceeded to preach from the Bible. Hearing someone clearly explain Scripture week after week exposed me to the way God speaks. It made me want to study the Bible. Those words, "Open your Bible," were a profound revelation.

Second the pastor preached a difficult passage. He was preaching through the Book of 1 Timothy, and on that Sunday morning he happened to be in chapter two where Paul says, "I do not permit a woman to teach or exercise authority over a man; rather, she should remain quiet" (v. 12). This passage was to me then—as it may be to you now—somewhat archaic, puzzling, and maybe even offensive. It's the kind of text most pastors skip.

But this pastor did something I admire: He preached hard passages. I will never forget what he said about this passage in which Paul restricts the role of women in the church. In effect, he said, "I don't really like this, and if God would have asked me what I thought before he wrote it, I would have told him to say something else. But this is God's Word. Trust that God knows what He is doing. Eventually we will come to realize the wisdom of what God is saying."

He then proceeded to explain the passage and connected it with the story of creation, as Paul does (vv. 13–14).

That story should serve a few purposes. Hopefully you go to a church where the Bible is taught. This will cause your faith to grow. It's not enough for a church to preach only the parts of the Bible they like. That can be the danger in focusing on selective or topical preaching and popular sermon series. Preaching what you like, what is comfortable, or what you think people want to hear is exactly what Paul warns against:

> I charge you in the presence of God and of Christ Jesus, who is to judge the living and the dead, and by his appearing and his kingdom: preach the word; be ready in season and out of season; reprove, rebuke, and exhort, with complete patience and teaching. For the time is coming when people will not endure sound teaching, but having itching ears they will accumulate for themselves teachers to suit their own passions, and will turn away from listening to the truth and wander off into myths.
> —2 Timothy 4:1–4

The phrase "itching ears" is a figure of speech. It means to tell people what they want to hear. This is the business model of Netflix and YouTube. They recommend things you are going to like, but that is unacceptable for the local church. God's Word is our daily bread, and God wants us to eat all of it (Matthew 4:4).

The Bible is often the source and solution of doubt.

The Bible is the source of doubt because it teaches things that are hard to hear. God's ways are not our ways (Isaiah 55:8–9). Jesus taught lessons His followers said were difficult and hard (John 6:60). Even the Apostle Peter says some of Paul's teachings were "hard to understand" (2 Peter 3:16). If Peter had a hard time understanding part of Paul's writing, don't be surprised if you do as well!

In one sense, the message of the Bible is simple. It can be summarized in one sentence: God created us and will forgive our sins if we believe that Jesus died and rose again to be our Savior and King. The entire Bible breaks down into four main themes—creation, fall, redemption, and restoration.

The Bible is simple, but that does not mean it is easy. It is a hard book. Enjoyable? Yes. Historically reliable? Absolutely. Inspired and inerrant? Indeed.

But it is a challenging book. Reading it will cause you to grow in the same way that working out at the gym gets you in shape—tough but worth it.

Doing something that is physically hard breaks down muscle cells so that new growth can occur. The process is painful. The pain keeps most people from growing.

Spiritual growth occurs in much the same way. Challenging ourselves to read more of Scripture and to think deeply in community about God's Word will break down our intellectual pride, expose our sins, and destroy our sense of self-sufficiency. This process is hard, but it will cause us to grow.

In *The Lego Movie*, an imaginary world is governed by evil Lord Business, whose goal is to distract people from his plans, which are (no spoiler here) *evil*. His two primary distractions are a song ("Everything Is Awesome") and a television show ("Where Are My Pants?"). Anytime someone notices how bad things are, Lord Business cues the music and the television show.

We prefer to be distracted because we prefer not to be confronted with hard truths.

If we are not careful, the local church can be a setting where the music boils down to "Everything Is Awesome" and the sermon an episode of "Where Are My Pants?" In other words, don't worry; just relax and enjoy.

In reality, Christianity is sometimes dangerous. The danger of Christianity is both physical and spiritual. Physically, people still die for following Jesus. Spiritually, following Jesus always requires us to die to self, turn from sins that come naturally, submit our thoughts to God, and many other challenging spiritual disciplines (Luke 9:23).

At some point Jesus is going to make you mad. You won't like that He is the potter and we are the clay (Isaiah 64:8). You won't like it when He says you have to forgive people or you won't be forgiven (Matthew 6:14–15). In the Bible's recordings of Jesus' time and words on earth, He talked more about hell than He talked about heaven.

At some point the Bible will make you mad. There is a right way and a wrong way to handle anger that stems from reading the Bible. You can stop reading, stop listening, stop going, and give up. That would be the wrong way to handle your anger.

Spiritual temper tantrums don't work. You cannot slam the door on God. Since He knows your thoughts even before you think them, you cannot give God the silent treatment.

Giving up on God because His Word made you mad is like quitting the gym because a workout made you sore. The right way to handle your anger during a crisis of faith is to go to Jesus. Keep reading. Talk it out in your church community. Ask your questions. Voice your doubts.

And all this leads us to the story of John the Baptist.

An Early Adopter

John the Baptist was to Christianity what today an early adopter is to Silicon Valley. He believed in Jesus before it was cool. Long before Jesus drew crowds, raised the dead, and fed the multitudes, John was on board.

The Bible tells us John was Jesus' cousin. When Mary announced her pregnancy to Elizabeth, who was pregnant herself with John at the time, the Holy Spirit filled John. While he was still in utero, John leaped for joy at the announcement that Mary was pregnant with the Lord (Luke 1:13–15; 39–45).

At the beginning of His public ministry, Jesus was baptized by John. At the time, John was baptizing people as a sign of repentance. Jesus showed up and asked to be baptized. John, of course, knew Jesus didn't need to repent. So why did He get baptized?

Jesus answered this question in Matthew 3:15. Jesus fulfilled all that righteousness requires. Jesus possessed perfect righteousness, but His acts of obedience demonstrated that righteousness. When people saw Jesus in the humble act of baptism, they would have thought, "This is a righteous man." Here is a man who obeys God.

John had a front-row seat to one of the most amazing moments in human history. As Jesus comes out of the water, the Spirit descends and the voice of the Father says, "This is my beloved Son, with whom I am well pleased" (v. 17). John was there! John the Baptist declared of Jesus, "Behold, the Lamb of God, who takes away the sin of the world!" (John 1:29).

John had his own ministry and drew large crowds (see Luke 3:7). Before anyone knew about Jesus, his cousin John was in demand. Despite his fame, John was humble. He knew he was unfit to carry Jesus' sandals (Matthew 3:11). In one of the most humble declarations in all of Scripture, John expressed the heart of worship, saying, "He [Jesus] must increase, but I must decrease" (John 3:30).

John was an influencer, but he was no people pleaser! This guy preached against sin and called out the people in power for their hypocrisy. He even spoke out publicly against the specific sins of specific rulers.

And that is how he ended up in prison.

Political Background

In 1979 the English punk band The Clash had a hit with the song, "I Fought the Law." The lyrics continue by saying, "And the law won." In one sense, that is what happened to John the Baptist. He fought the law, and the law won.

When Jesus was alive, Israel was under Roman rule. From about 4 BC to AD 39, a man named Herod Antipas ruled over Galilee. Herod had two main jobs: maintain order and collect taxes.

Named after his father Herod the Great (who tried to kill the newborn Jesus), Herod Antipas had a brother named Philip. In the Gospel of Matthew, it says Philip had a wife named Herodias. At some point, Philip and Herodias were divorced, and Herod Antipas married his brother's ex-wife, Herodias.

Matthew tells us John spoke out about the affair, saying, "It is against God's law for you to marry her" (Matthew 14:4 NLT). John didn't just say this once! He persistently confronted Herod about his sin (v. 4).

Imagine you are a Roman ruler. You have been publicly humiliated by an itinerant desert preacher. The preacher is Jewish, and you rule over the Jews. Wouldn't your first instinct be to have the preacher arrested and then killed? That's exactly what Herod wanted to do: "Herod wanted to kill John" (v. 5 NLT).

Here is the problem: A Roman ruler had to keep order. Remember that John the Baptist was popular. Upset a crowd, and you might have a riot. And so, sensing public opinion was not on his side, Herod settled for arresting John.

News about Jesus

Hollywood has made a lot of prison movies, but my favorite is *The Shawshank Redemption*, featuring Tim Robbins playing the unjustly imprisoned Andy Dufresne. He befriends seasoned inmate Ellis "Red" Redding, played by the great Morgan Freeman. The two become friends because Red is the kind of guy who can get you things in prison.

Meanwhile Andy becomes indispensable to the sadistic and hypocritical prison warden. His work gets him special perks. Between Red and the warden, Andy is able to survive.

A Roman prison was different from the prisons you see on television or in movies. Rome's job was to imprison you. If you wanted to stay alive, you needed friends who would bring you food, care for you, and keep up your spirits.

For this reason, it says in the Gospel of Luke, that John was able to visit with his disciples. They likely brought him food and provided basic care for John. And, it stands to reason, they would have brought news about what was going on in the outside world. The latest news about his family. While John (the once-famous baptizer) was in prison, his cousin Jesus was growing in popularity.

The author and singer Morrissey wrote a song, and the title captures the nature of jealousy: "We Hate It When Our Friends Become Successful." John used to be the star, and now he has been upstaged. But John wanted Jesus to take the spotlight. Then again, fame is probably hard to relinquish.

What we know is that while in prison John had a crisis of faith. We know this because when his disciples came to visit him, John sent a message through them back to Jesus. John instructed them to ask Jesus a revealing question: "Are you the one who is to come, or shall we look for another?" (Luke 7:20).

John doubted what he knew to be true. John had already settled the question of Jesus' identity. He had declared it to the masses: This is the Lamb of God! He had heard the voice of God: This is My beloved Son!

What happened to John? He asked a question to which he already knew the answer. In a crisis of faith, to borrow from the American folk-poet Blaze Foley, we look for answers to questions we already know.

Circumstances and Doubt

Doubt is often a product of circumstances. What we profess in the light we question in the dark. Call it hypocrisy. Call it sin. Call it fallen human nature. Whatever happened to John is something to which we can all relate.

There is a logic to John's doubt. Doubt, after all, is not wholly irrational.

John believes Jesus is the Messiah. The Messiah is going to free His people. He is going to pay for their sins, kick out the Romans, restore the covenant blessings, and institute shalom.

Jesus is doing all kinds of great things John is hearing about in prison. The sick being healed! The hungry fed! The blind receiving sight! Even the dead are raised!

So many good things happening to so many other people.

You can imagine John thinking to himself, "Why am I in prison? Where are You, Jesus? Are You even the Messiah? Should I be looking for someone else? Can You *really* save?"

We all know this feeling. Your friend's social media feed contains pictures of their sonogram when you and your spouse cannot get pregnant. A friend shares a praise for a new job at church, and you share a prayer request because you just got laid off. Someone on Twitter shares an anniversary picture, and you're going through a divorce.

Where are You, Jesus? Are You even the Messiah? Should I be looking for someone else?

You may have heard that there is no such thing as an atheist in a foxhole. This is simply not true. Christian author C. S. Lewis was an atheist in a foxhole during World War I. He went into the foxholes and trenches of wartime France as an atheist, and he came out an atheist just the same.

His poetry during his time in Riez du Vinage speaks to his unbelief: "Come let us curse our Master ere we die / For all our hopes in endless ruin lie." Even after being seriously wounded, Lewis refused to return to the faith of his youth, or as he put it then, to fall "back into the most childish superstitions."

Life's battlefields (both literally and figuratively) possess no magic power to transform unbelief into faith. In the film adaptation of Erich Maria Remarque's novel *All Quiet on the Western Front* (1928) the character Paul describes soldiers returning from the Great War as "weary, broken, burnt out, rootless, and without hope."

War is not revival. Kurt Vonnegut says the whole business of atheists and foxholes is an argument against foxholes. In his book *Hocus Pocus*, he says anyone who says there are no atheists in foxholes has never visited a foxhole.

Suffering has limitations. It can expose the true self, but it cannot create the true self. In suffering, the believing self is trying to hold on to faith. Salvation is a supernatural act, and only God can shape good character. Faith is a gift of God. There is nothing inherently faith-producing about hardships. Everyone suffers, but not everyone receives the gift of faith.

Suffering is not a magical event that turns barbed wire into rainbows. It is the cold and inhospitable testing ground of the self. It strengthens and reveals what is already within.

Suffering is like age. Wisdom does not come automatically with age. There are old fools and wise youth, although in general, you're more likely to find wisdom in a nursing home than a skate park. Nevertheless, wisdom is not inherent to age just as faith is not inherent to suffering. Both come to the person who seeks God.

The Christian hope is that God is with us in suffering and uses suffering for our good and His glory. He is the Good Shepherd who tends to us in the Valley of the Shadow of Death. In fact, God in Christ has gone before us through the veil. He has already crossed the river and waits for us on the other side. Jesus says, "Take heart; I have overcome the world" (John 16:33).

God doesn't just go with us in suffering; He promises to see us through. Jude says God is able to keep us from falling (Jude 1:24). Jesus promises not to lose even a single sheep (John 6:39). He stakes His word on every believer persevering to the end.

His power will prevail over our doubt. Grace wins for those who receive it. Doubt will not have the final say.

A Merciful Response

We see this powerful truth in the unfolding story of John the Baptist in prison. Jesus gets John's message of teetering faith and sends a response. The message Jesus sends back to John is perplexing, merciful, and instructive:

> Go and tell John what you have seen and heard: the blind receive their sight, the lame walk, lepers are cleansed, and the deaf hear, the dead are raised up, the poor have good news preached to them. And blessed is the one who is not offended by me. —Luke 7:22–23

Why is this perplexing? Because Jesus doesn't really answer the question. If I had been John, I would have wanted a one-word answer: Yes.

Yes, I am the Messiah.

John didn't get that message. Easy answers don't challenge our faith. Unchallenged faith doesn't grow. Jesus want us to grow through the trials, not just make it through.

John didn't get a simple answer. In a crisis of faith, there are rarely simple answers. Some answers never come, others are complex, and sometimes the answers are just not what we want to hear.

Notice, however, that Jesus does not chastise John for his doubt. Jesus doesn't respond harshly to John. He doesn't say "Get it together, John" or "I'm too busy for this, John." Jesus responds mercifully to those who doubt.

Jesus blesses John: "Blessed is the one who is not offended by me." Faith isn't offended when God allows you to suffer. Jesus is gentle and straightforward. He reminds John that his suffering has a purpose. Jesus does not join in John's panic. He can sympathize with our suffering, but He cannot empathize with our unbelief. Jesus is both sinless and merciful to sinners.

In a powerful demonstration of mercy, Jesus blesses John. Our doubt does not deserve a blessing. This act of Jesus is a measure of grace.

In *Les Misérables*, author Victor Hugo tells a redemption story about a changed man named Jean Valjean. After being released from prison, Valjean is given a prison number, and his identity is consumed by his failure. He is now known only as prisoner 24601 and given a prison identification card, which effectively keeps him from finding work or even a place to stay.

Desperate and angry, Valjean is allowed to stay in the home of a minister, Bishop Myriel. In the middle of the night, Valjean steals silver from the Bishop's home and is caught by the police, who return him to the Bishop's house to collect a statement. When they arrive, the Bishop doesn't incriminate Valjean to the police. Instead he tells the police he gave the stolen items to Valjean and in fact adds to the silver Valjean took.

After the police leave, Valjean and the Bishop are alone. Valjean is confused by grace. Never before has he been pardoned. The sense of forgiveness is totally foreign. To his bewilderment, the Bishop blesses Valjean:

> Jean Valjean was like a man on the point of fainting. The Bishop drew near to him and said in a low voice: "Do not forget, never forget, that you have promised to use this money in becoming an honest man." Jean Valjean, who had no recollection of ever having promised anything, remained speechless. The Bishop had emphasized the words when he uttered them. He resumed with solemnity: "Jean Valjean, my brother, you no longer belong to evil, but to good. It is your soul that I buy from you; I withdraw it from black thoughts and the spirit of perdition, and I give it to God."

In the musical, the song that depicts this scene features Valjean responding to the unexpected blessing of the Bishop by tearing up his prisoner identification card, the symbol of his past and ongoing doubts, and declaring his name (Jean Valjean) over his prisoner identification number (24601).

John wants to know for sure that Jesus is the Messiah. Jesus does that for John. But more than that, Jesus reminds John of his belief.

Don't be offended, John. Keep believing.

It is safe for doubters to draw near to God. It is a sad yet common mistake for believers to run from God in times of doubt, the very times we need Him most. Adam and Eve ran away from God in the Garden when they realized they had sinned, and we have been running ever since.

Believers battle the primal urge of Eden: to run and hide from God in our shame and in our failure. To run from the only person who can help us.

Yet in the Garden of Eden, God becomes the first missionary and goes after Adam and Eve in order to save them. Jesus becomes the incarnate Savior in pursuit of fallen humanity. By grace we stop running, turn around, and run toward God.

Here is the point: In your doubt and unbelief go to Jesus. You will find mercy. Don't run from Him, His people, His Word, or His Spirit. When doubters go to Jesus they are blessed.

Good Advice

Jesus has more than a blessing for John. He has great advice. Remember the response Jesus gives? The blind receive sight? Lepers are cleansed? The deaf hear? The dead are raised?

John asked, "Are you the one to come?" In other words, are You the Messiah? John wants confirmation that it makes sense to keep believing.

Doubt is faith looking for answers. You don't go looking for something unless you think it exists. The good news is that God is willing to remind us why it makes sense to believe.

This is exactly what Jesus does in His response to John.

The list of miracles Jesus recites for John is straight from the Old Testament. Jesus is quoting Scripture to John. Scripture is our weapon against doubt.

About seven hundred years before Jesus was born, God spoke through a prophet named Isaiah. Through Isaiah, God promised He would not abandon His people but would come to them and bring salvation. God's people would know the Messiah because He would perform certain miracles. Below is the passage from Isaiah that Jesus quoted in His response to John:

> Strengthen the weak hands, and make firm the feeble knees. Say to those who have an anxious heart, "Be strong; fear not! Behold, your God will come with vengeance, with the recompense of God. He will come and save you." Then the eyes of the blind shall be opened, and the ears of the deaf unstopped; then shall the lame man leap like a deer, and the tongue of the mute sing for joy. For waters break forth in the wilderness, and streams in the desert; the burning sand shall become a pool, and the thirsty ground springs of water; in the haunt of jackals, where they lie down, the grass shall become reeds and rushes.
> —Isaiah 35:3–7

Jesus is strengthening John's weak-handed and wobbly-kneed faith with Scripture. One way we get through a crisis of faith is by remembering what God has said. Looking at God's past faithfulness is one reason it makes sense to continue trusting Him.

God said through Isaiah that He would come and save His people. When He did, they would know it! Certain things would happen. Jesus was reminding John in prison that He was the Messiah. He was Immanuel (God with us).

There is something to be said for the concept of blind faith. Danish existentialist philosopher Søren Kierkegaard wrote in his 1847 book *Uplifting Discourses in Various Spirits* that "faith sees best in the dark." Jesus put it this way: "Blessed are those who have not seen and yet have believed" (John 20:29). There is something about the determination of faith against all (apparent) odds that is inspiring.

The nineteen-eighties were a great time for inspirational movies. *Rocky IV* featured the unlikely boxing victory of Rocky over Soviet machine Ivan Drago. *The Karate Kid* had Daniel winning over Cobra-Kai wunderkind Johnny Lawrence. These movies were inspiring because things seemed hopeless. In storytelling, the greater the conflict, the sweeter the resolution.

John is in prison. The Romans are ruling. The religious leaders are hypocrites. Things look really bad. John starts to doubt, and Jesus reminds him of an ancient passage that is being fulfilled.

The message is clear: Remember what God has said. Go back to what you know. In times of doubt, focusing on what you don't know will cause your doubt to grow. Focusing on what you know will cause faith to grow.

A crisis of faith often starts when a person fixates on the unknown. Will I get into college? Will I get married? Will I get a promotion? What is going to happen with the economy? Focusing on what you don't know will worsen the crisis of faith.

John did not know if he would get out of prison. Jesus doesn't answer all of John's unspoken questions. There are many things in this life we will never know. But if we choose to focus on what we do know, then we can grow in faith and find peace in times of doubt.

The church cannot tell you what your health will be like next year. No pastor can predict your future. No televangelist can guarantee you will be richer next year, no matter how much money you send to their ministry. In times of doubt, reaching for false hope worsens the crisis of faith. False teachers and snake oil salesman prey on doubting Christians desperate for hope, but they cannot deliver.

Real hope is found by doubting Christians who remember what God has said in His Word. Immerse yourself in His story, and your focus will shift from you (where it doesn't belong) to Him (where it does belong). Times of doubt often result from shattered pride. When the ego takes a hit, the illusion of self-importance and self-sufficiency is exposed. Anything from a breakup to a bad day can trigger vulnerability. Once exposed, we overreact by questioning everything.

Doubt is often an emotional overreaction to the wounded ego. A crisis of faith should move you to the point where you abandon hope in self and pursue God. If you are angry at God, at least you are thinking about God. If you are doubting His Word, at least you are engaged. Doubt is a great benefit when it causes you to deny yourself and look outward and upward where there are answers.

G. K. Chesterton makes this point when he says in *The Book of Job*, "In dealing with the arrogant asserter of doubt . . . the right method is to tell him to go on doubting, to doubt a little more, to doubt every day newer and wilder things in the universe, until at last, by some strange enlightenment, he may begin to doubt himself."

The mantra of modern secularism is to trust thyself, listen to thyself, and heal thyself. The Christian confessions respond differently at each point. Doubt thyself and trust God. Preach to thyself. Thou art the problem and not the solution. It has long been repeated that *The Times* once sent a simple question to famous authors, "What's wrong with the world today?" It is purported Chesterton humbly replied, "I am."

Doubt is a knife that, when turned inward, is of great benefit. It causes pride to break like a fever and leaves us in a sweat of clarity where we can see our weakness and God's faithfulness and can get our bearing in God's Word. Going through a time of doubt properly can produce a kind of spiritual renewal and rededication.

The antidote to the nausea of doubt is the faithfulness of God. We learn about God's faithfulness from the Old and New Testaments. Together they form a single coherent story about who God is, what God has done, and what God will do. The story of our lives is fraught with uncertainty. Faith grows when we anchor our lives to the story of God's glory revealed in Scripture.

More to the Story

After John received Jesus' message he had all he needed to faithfully endure his trial to the end. Jesus did not pamper him with false promises. He dignified John by speaking directly to his doubt with the true substance of faith: the Word of God. Our impulse in dealing with doubt is often to revert to pretend faith expressed in empty platitudes like, "It's all going to be okay," and, "I know you can do it."

Empty words and hollow platitudes worsen and prolong doubt. It is one thing to doubt what is true. It is another thing to say something and pretend it is true. We are not little gods who can speak reality into existence. Our words do not create reality. Only God has the power to create reality with His words and thoughts.

John never got out of prison. Remember Herod Antipas, the ruler John rebuked for his adultery with Herodias? Turns out Herodias had a daughter, who one night at a party performed a dance for Herod.

Wanting to honor her and make a show of his wealth, he offered his daughter almost half his kingdom. The girl went to her mother, Herodias, to find out what kind of request she should make. Undoubtedly still angry about her public humiliation, Herodias instructed the girl to ask for the head of John the Baptist on a platter. Her wish was the king's command, and Herod had John's head cut off. We are told that John's disciples came and took the body, and when Jesus heard what had happened, He withdrew to the wilderness in mourning. (See Matthew 14; Mark 6; and Luke 9.)

Jesus loved His cousin John.

God's love does not keep us from suffering. God's goal is our holiness, not our comfort. God wants to grow our faith, not our ease. John never got out of prison, but his suffering was not wasted.

The Mystery of Providence in Suffering

How did God use John's suffering? After John was beheaded, Herod thought he had solved a problem. But in Luke 9, it says:

> Now Herod the tetrarch heard about all that was happening, and he was perplexed, because it was said by some that John had been raised from the dead, by some that Elijah had appeared, and by others that one of the prophets of old had risen. Herod said, "John I beheaded, but who is this about whom I hear such things?" And he sought to see him. —Luke 9:7–9

In a twist to the story, Herod pays attention to Jesus because John was martyred. Jesus, by this time, was more popular than John had been, and Herod was hearing stories. The stories about Jesus reminded Herod of John. Who else could do these miracles? Had John risen from the dead? It says Herod was perplexed. The original Greek word used here (*diaporeó*) can be translated as "troubled." John was troubled in prison, and Jesus combatted his doubt with God's Word. Herod was troubled and went looking for Jesus.

John's suffering contributes to the glory and fame of Jesus.

Herod may never have paid attention to Jesus had it not been for John's suffering. Herod goes on to play a significant role in the redemption mission of Jesus. After his arrest and appearance before the Jewish priests and scribes, Pilate sends Jesus to Herod, because Herod was over the region of Galilee, where Jesus was from (Luke 23:6–12). Herod questions Jesus and demands He perform a miracle, but Jesus will not talk, and Jesus refuses to perform like a trained animal. This in itself fulfills a prophesy in Isaiah, which says, "He was oppressed, and he was afflicted, yet he opened not his mouth" (Isaiah 53:7).

Herod and his goons respond to Jesus like classic bullies, mocking Him and dressing Him in royal clothing. They think it is funny Jesus would be a king. The joke sticks. Jesus is sent back to Pilate, who delivers Him to be crucified. Pilate and Herod were enemies, but that day, they became friends (Luke 23:12).

John had no idea how his momentary light afflictions would produce an eternal weight of glory (2 Corinthians 4:17–18) through the death of Jesus for sinners. In times of doubt, go to God's Word, and remember that God will use your suffering in profound and mysterious ways. You do not know who is watching or how God will leverage your hardships for His glory and your good. There will be invisible ripple effects to your persistent faith.

Doubt Doesn't Define You

A short time after Jesus answered John, Jesus delivers a message about the importance of John's role:

> When John's messengers had gone, Jesus began to speak to the crowds concerning John: "What did you go out into the wilderness to see? A reed shaken by the wind? What then did you go out to see? A man dressed in soft clothing? Behold, those who are dressed in splendid clothing and live in luxury are in kings' courts. What then did you go out to see? A prophet? Yes, I tell you, and more than a prophet. This is he of whom it is written, 'Behold, I send my messenger before your face, who will prepare your way before you.' I tell you, among those born of women none is greater than John. Yet the one who is least in the kingdom of God is greater than he." —Luke 7:24–28

Jesus thinks highly of John. He is no coward, no reed shaken by the wind. His doubt doesn't make him weak. No soft clothing for John. In

Great Expectations, Charles Dickens writes, "We need never be ashamed of our tears." Real men cry too. Biblical manliness is not stoic emotionlessness, nor is genuine faith unassailable. John believes and doubts. He goes to Jesus for reassurance. Jesus affirms him as a great man.

A crisis of faith exposes the fact that you are not a spiritual superhero. There is no Iron Man suit for the believer. In those moments when your frailty and fallen humanity are exposed, it is a mistake to overreact and think that somehow you've blown it or that you don't believe. Moments of doubt, days of doubt, do not cancel out genuine decisions of faith, real repentance, and a life of commitment to Jesus. Our doubt, and especially sinful decisions made in times of doubt, have real and lasting consequences. Those consequences, however, do not negate our adoption into God's family. Doubt does not erase your last name.

Jesus doesn't define John by his moment of doubt but by his life of faith. What a testament to God's grace. Jude says we are to have mercy on doubters amongst us, meaning that the church is to be merciful to its members in a crisis of faith. Help each other survive a crisis of faith.

In a crisis of faith, sometimes the thing you doubt most is whether or not you have faith at all. Am I even a believer? If I am a believer, how can I doubt? Remember that faith is God's irrevocable gift (Ephesians 2:8–10). Once given it cannot be taken away; not even by you. Not even you can snatch you from God's hand (John 10:28–30).

Decide to Keep Believing

In his excellent book *Moral Choices,* ethicist Scott Rae lists steps to making a moral decision. A wise person gathers the facts, determines the relevant ethical issues and virtues, compares the alternatives, and considers consequences. The final step to this process is crucial: *make a decision.*

You cannot deliberate forever. At some point you have to decide to keep believing, to persist in faith. Even with certain unanswered questions, Christianity makes more sense than the alternatives. No worldview or philosophical system will deliver absolute certainty. Everyone has faith in something or someone. To quote the title of the lead track from Bob Dylan's album *Slow Train Coming,* you "Gotta Serve Somebody."

Faith may not be *from* you, but it belongs *to you*. God is the source of our faith, but it becomes our faith. We exercise a redeemed will over our faith. It is our responsibility to guide, defend, and protect the precious gift of faith. We can and should will to believe, desire to believe, fight for faith, and preach to ourselves.

Jude expresses the paradox of God's sovereignty and our responsibility at the end of his letter in the Bible. In one verse he says, "Keep yourselves in the love of God" (Jude 1:21), and only a few verses later say God is "able to keep you from stumbling and to present you blameless before the presence of His glory with great joy" (v. 24).

Which is it? Do we keep ourselves or does God keep us? In a sense, it is both. God is ultimately the one who keeps us, but He uses the means of our dogged faith, our determination to persist in belief, and our refusal to give in to our doubts.

The Potter uses the clay.

Conclusion

In a crisis of faith, it is a mistake to listen to yourself. Your inner doubts will fixate on the unknown. To make it through a crisis of faith, you must preach to yourself. Remember what you know in order to build faith. Go to God's Word, and get your bearings. Decide to keep believing, and take ownership of your faith.

Chapter 3

Doubting Thomas: Unless I See

So far we have seen that faith is like a dimmer switch. Sometimes faith is bright and strong, other times it is weak and dim. Faith is not the absence of doubt, and doubt is not the absence of faith.

In this chapter we will see that doubt often unfolds in stages. It will help you to know these stages and to anticipate common responses to doubt. In order to develop a strategy for dealing with doubt, we must first understand our common reactions to the nausea of unbelief.

Stages of Doubt

Denial, anger, bargaining, depression, and acceptance. Sound familiar? These are the five stages of grief espoused by psychiatrist Elisabeth Kübler-Ross in her 1969 book *On Death and Dying*, in which her main thesis is that grief—how people cope with illness and dying—doesn't just happen at once, nor is it a linear progression. There is a process to grief, and understanding the process makes a person more capable of navigating loss in a healthy manner.

Doubt, like grief, has a process. You might even say that doubt is a kind of grief. Like grief, doubt is the complicated reaction to loss. In the case of grief, it is the loss of a person. In the case of doubt, it is the loss of a thing.

In doubt we lose certainty.

Philosopher René Descartes wrote a book called *Meditation on First Philosophy* in which he established criteria for belief that has had seismic repercussions. His revolutionary idea (referred to as the Cartesian Revolution) is that foundational beliefs must be inscrutable. In other words, your beliefs must be based upon something that is beyond doubt. Not reasonable doubt, mind you; doubt itself.

So if you can doubt something, that thing cannot be the foundation of your worldview. In a brilliant (if misguided) intellectual exercise, Descartes sits in his study and doubts everything people base their knowledge upon—God, math, and the world of sensation (i.e., the things you see, touch, taste, and smell).

After doubting all these things, he concludes that there is one thing he cannot doubt: he exists. After all, he is doubting! Doubting is a form of thought, and if he is doubting, then he is thinking, and if he is thinking, then he exists. You probably know Descartes's famous dictum: I think, therefore I am.

At the end of this thought experiment, Descartes concludes that a person's existence is the one thing that can be known beyond doubt, and can therefore serve as a foundation of knowledge.

This kind of doubt is called methodological doubt. It is the kind of doubt that treats the world as guilty until proven innocent. It assumes something doesn't exist until someone proves it does. This kind of doubt leads to skepticism.

A skeptic is someone whose starting point is doubt. Of course, no one can live this way. A skeptic usually reserves their doubt for certain things, like God. Skeptics usually apply their skepticism when convenient—not to beliefs about memory or perception but to God and miracles.

Descartes set a bar for belief that played to skepticism. If knowledge has zero room for doubt, then we can know very little directly. Now you might be thinking, "What does this have to do with faith? After all, faith is about beliefs, not knowledge."

Actually, any of your true beliefs about the world can count as knowledge. Having good reasons for your beliefs and practicing intellectual virtue (open-mindedness, humility, courage, etc.) gives you confidence to hold your beliefs strongly. Beliefs about God, who should be president, climate change, and what you ate for lunch yesterday are all beliefs that can be known with varying levels of confidence corresponding to reason, evidence, and the intellectual virtue.

Now, think about something you believe. For instance, who do you believe was your fourth grade teacher? Got the answer? I know mine. I can remember him as though it were yesterday because he told stories about his service in Vietnam.

Who was yours? How did you arrive at the belief? Maybe you remember, or maybe you had to ask your siblings or a parent. Or perhaps you looked it up in an old school annual. Your belief about your fourth grade teacher comes from somewhere, either memory, testimony, or pictures.

But you could be wrong. You could remember wrongly, or your parents could misremember. Your annual could be wrong! Or worse, what if someone doctored the annual to confuse you? Pictures can be edited, editors can get things wrong, people can misremember.

Do you really know the name of your fourth grade teacher?

Of course you do! But that little exercise made you realize that all beliefs can be doubted, even simple beliefs like what you ate for lunch yesterday. Sometimes we get it wrong, but most of the time, our memory, senses, and powers of induction and deduction work pretty reliably. God designed us to understand and know the world He made.

All this to say that you can know something and still be able to doubt that belief. I'm pretty confident that I ate Indian food for lunch yesterday, but it's possible I could be wrong. Skepticism defies common sense and everyday life; it's not the way God created us to function and get things done!

Descartes was wrong about knowledge and the need for certainty. Unfortunately, many of us fall prey to his error in regard to faith. In college, professors like to give students reasons to doubt belief in God. They rarely provide fair counterreasons for faith in God. Even more rarely do they apply those same doubts to beliefs about science, politics, and other areas of study.

In other words, when it comes to God, there is a double standard. Atheists ridicule Christians for invoking God to explain things we otherwise cannot explain, such as the origin of the universe. This is called

God of the gaps. But these same atheists have no problem talking about dark matter, a theoretical entity invoked to bridge the gap between what is known and what is unknown. Like God, dark matter is postulated to make sense of what we otherwise cannot explain.

When it comes to God there are three kinds of people: believers, skeptics, and scoffers.[1] Believers look for reasons to keep believing. Skeptics look for reasons to doubt. Scoffers don't seriously consider the evidence or arguments and make fun of people who believe.

Skeptics and scoffers require a different response from believers. Scoffers are to be avoided and will be judged (Psalm 1:1). Scoffers are fools (Psalm 14:1) and an abomination to humankind (Proverbs 24:9). Christians should engage skeptics and avoid scoffers.

There is a kind of skepticism that is good. Socrates is purported to have said that the unexamined life is not worth living. The Greek word *skepsis* means to investigate. Socrates does not mean, like Descartes, that knowledge requires certainty. The examined life is one in which a wise person investigates his or her beliefs and considers reason and evidence.

If you think knowledge requires certainty, then a crisis of faith is like grief. You are mourning the loss of certainty.

At first you get angry. Angry at your college professor, angry at the passage of Scripture that has made you mad, or even angry at God. Anger is a natural response to feeling as though the rug has been pulled out from under your feet.

After anger, you bargain. If God shows you a sign, then you'll keep believing. If you can find an argument against your professor, then you'll keep going to church. If God will heal your sick child, then you will never doubt God again.

In other words, a quid pro quo.

Once doubt has expressed itself in anger and done some bargaining, then comes depression. Depression makes sense in the wake of doubt because usually you don't get a miracle. There are scenes in the Bible when Paul and Silas are in jail singing and praising God, and then God sends an earthquake to break them out of jail. Hallelujah!

---

[1] I am indebted to my friend Dr. Ben Arbour for his contribution to this chapter in helping me to see the distinction between believers, skeptics, and scoffers. Ben is a Christian philosopher, with whom I have collaborated on writing projects such as *Idealism and Christian Philosophy*.

Later in Acts, Paul is in prison and spends two years there, no doubt singing and praising God just like before, only this time, no miracle.

Let's be honest; usually you don't get a miracle. In the Old Testament, when Israel was going into the Promised Land it was filled with enemies that God commanded Israel to defeat. At one city named Jericho, God caused the walls to fall down with some simple marching and music. Most of the other times, Israel just had to fight. God was always at work, but His work didn't always look like a miracle.

Unsuccessful bargaining and the lack of a miracle can result in depression. Does God even love me? Does anyone love me? You don't want to get out of bed. You don't want to talk to anyone. You don't want to go to class, or work, or church.

A person in the depression stage of a crisis of faith often doesn't want to talk about it anymore. They quit reading books, quit seeking advice or counsel, and resign themselves to their new normal. Not every question can be answered. Every belief can be doubted. Knowledge isn't bulletproof.

Christians experience doubt in stages because it is a kind of loss. Something is gone. Ultimately you have two choices. You can choose to accept it and move forward or try to recover what has been lost. Moving forward means accepting a new normal. Life looks different, but it is still life, and it is still worth living.

The new normal is that you will have questions no one can answer. There will be doctrines that (to your liking) are insufficiently clear or unresolved. For every argument, there is a counterargument. Doubt is like a shadow. It goes where you go.

Acceptance is the final stage.

Let me be clear. Christianity has plenty of answers. There are good arguments for belief in God. There is nothing like the historical proof for the resurrection in any other religion. We have more evidence for the Bible than any other book of antiquity. Christianity makes more sense of the world than atheism, agnosticism, or any other system of belief. Hands down, Christianity makes sense. It is rational. It is worth believing. It is true.

Doubt is like Whac-A-Mole. There is always some new doubt to combat. One goes down, and another comes up.

Apologetics is like looking under the bed for a monster. Do you remember being a kid and having the crippling fear that a monster was under the bed or in the closet? You cried out, or went to get your parents, and they would comfort you by turning on the lights and opening the closet door to look under the bed. Nothing there!

Hallelujah!

And then they leave. Turn out the lights. What if the monster hides when the light is on? What if the monster can only be seen by peculiar children like you? What if the monster moved from the closet to under the bed when you weren't looking? Maybe my parents are wrong. What do they know, anyway?

No amount of evidence will quiet the sinful discomfort of unbelief.

Doubt is loss. Something is gone. Life goes on, only different.

And better.

Enter Thomas

Have you ever had a nickname? Sometimes we get nicknames that are not flattering. In Christianity, Thomas is known popularly as Doubting Thomas because of an incident in which he doubted Jesus. The good news is that this incident of doubt—his crisis of faith—is instructive for us. Thomas helps us see the value of doubt in strengthening faith.

The story goes that Jesus had risen from the dead. Lots of people had seen Him, but not Thomas. Isn't that how it goes? Everyone has seen a miracle but me. Everyone has heard God's voice except me. We have all felt left out.

Thomas makes a bargain, typical grief processing. He plays the part of the skeptic. He has a David Hume, Charles Darwin, Bill Nye the Science Guy intensity of unbelief. Seeing Jesus perform miracles isn't enough for Thomas. Seeing Jesus risen from the dead isn't enough for Thomas. No, Thomas demands to see *and touch* the nail imprints on the resurrected body of Jesus.

That is some next level doubt. The amazing thing is that Jesus says, "Okay." Here is the scene from the Gospel of John:

Now Thomas, one of the twelve, called the Twin, was not with them when Jesus came. So the other disciples told him,

"We have seen the Lord." But he said to them, "Unless I see in his hands the mark of the nails, and place my finger into the mark of the nails, and place my hand into his side, I will never believe." Eight days later, his disciples were inside again, and Thomas was with them. Although the doors were locked, Jesus came and stood among them and said, "Peace be with you." Then he said to Thomas, "Put your finger here, and see my hands; and put out your hand, and place it in my side. Do not disbelieve, but believe." Thomas answered him, "My Lord and my God!" Jesus said to him, "Have you believed because you have seen me? Blessed are those who have not seen and yet have believed." —John 20:24–29

Thomas was not always Doubting Thomas. You cannot chalk unbelief up to personality or disposition. Earlier in the Gospel of John, Thomas was with Jesus and the disciples when they received news that their friend Lazarus was dying. Jesus said He was going to be with Lazarus. It was risky going to be with someone who was dying. You were likely to contract their illness and die with them! Once Jesus declared His intention to go and be with Lazarus, Thomas said, "Let us also go, that we may die with him" (John 11:16).

Thomas didn't always doubt. At times he exhibited strong faith. As with Thomas, our doubt cannot be dismissed merely as a byproduct of personality, disposition, temperament, genetics, or chemistry. It is, most fundamentally, a spiritual ailment. Otherwise courageous Christians can find themselves doubting, making demands, and bargaining with God.

Bargaining Doubt

Just because Thomas doubts does not mean doubt is good. It isn't. All the stories in the Bible are true, but not all stories in the Bible are prescriptive. Reading a story in the Bible in the context of the book in which it was written, and in the context of the message of the Bible as a whole, reveals the meaning and point of the story. In the case of Thomas, the point is not that we should doubt but rather that we should believe.

But in a crisis of faith, such as the one Thomas was having, there are lessons to be learned about the right (and wrong) way to deal with doubt.

In terms of mistakes, Thomas models the danger of bargaining with God in times of doubt. A bargain (or negotiation) is a kind of demand. It reveals a lack of faith. The Bible is filled with Doubting Thomas figures who doubted and whose doubt was expressed in bargaining.

Long before Thomas there was Gideon. God instructed Gideon to take military action against the enemies of Israel, and He promised their success. Gideon did not respond in faith-filled obedience but in handwringing doubt. He asked God (respectfully) for a sign *and then* he would be happy to obey. (See Judges 6:36–40).

Asking God for signs signals our doubt, lack of faith, and general distrust in God. It is seeking to negotiate a transaction with God, who needs nothing and holds all the cards. Jesus says that a wicked and adulterous generation demands a sign (Matthew 16:4).

Making demands of God as a condition of faith, or obedience, is presumptive. We are not in a position to bargain with God. Bargaining implies we have something to offer, when in fact, we don't. We have neither the will to believe nor the faith required. We need it all from God.

Faith and Evidence

It is interesting that Jesus commands Thomas to believe and not doubt after He presented Himself as the evidence for faith. God is not opposed to evidence, and biblical faith is reasonable. Acts 1:3 says Jesus presented Himself alive with many *proofs*.

There is no shame in looking for evidence that supports the truthfulness of Scripture. Saint Anselm, an eleventh century Christian philosopher and theologian, wrote a book called *Proslogion* in which he made arguments for God's existence. Anselm's motto was *fides quaerens intellectum*, which means faith seeking understanding. Reason can never replace faith, but faith is never divorced from reason.

The resurrection of Jesus is supported by evidence and proof. God designed it that way. When doubt arises, looking for evidence that supports the truthfulness of Scripture is a reasonable pursuit.

The Apostle John wrote an epistle in which he talked about having seen and touched Jesus. He says, speaking of Jesus:

That which was from the beginning, which we have heard, which we have seen with our eyes, which we looked upon and have touched with our hands, concerning the word of life—the life was made manifest, and we have seen it, and testify to it and proclaim to you the eternal life, which was with the Father and was made manifest to us. —1 John 1:1–2

It would be a mistake to suppose that the pursuit of evidence and arguments in support of Christianity is always an indication of doubt. It is often evidence of faith: faith seeking understanding.

Biblical faith is not blind faith. God is not silent, and He is not hiding. He speaks through His Word, and in Christ He has made Himself known. Nature declares His glory (Psalm 19:1), the church is a pillar of the truth (1 Timothy 3:15), and events in history are a testimony to His sovereign decrees (Job 1:21–22).

The arguments in defense of God's existence, the historical proofs that confirm the historicity of Scripture, and the failure of arguments and evidence against God and His Word are faith-building. While these proofs and arguments are not necessary for faith, they can be a means of reviving faith in times of spiritual crisis.

The fight for faith is like mixed martial arts (MMA). In MMA, the fighter uses a mixture of styles to beat his opponent. Unlike boxing, where kicks are prohibited, MMA fighters can kick, punch, knee, grapple, choke, and just about anything else (with a few exceptions). Despite my own opposition to the sport, it serves as a helpful analogy to faith fighting doubt.

All you need is the Bible, but that is not all you have. You have a local church filled with people who have wrestled with similar doubts and questions. You have two thousand years of Christian theologians and philosophers who have written extensively on just about every conceivable topic. You can study "the wager" by Blaise Pascal, the moral argument by C. S. Lewis, and the divine language argument of George Berkeley. You can read about the evidence for creation from specified complexity and how evolution, if true, would negate naturalism.

The above concepts may be foreign to you, but there are arguments, proofs, evidence, and reason for believing in the Bible. A crisis of faith is a cage match during which different maneuvers will be required at different stages in the fight. You prepare yourself by knowing as many moves as you can master, and you make it through a crisis of faith by throwing everything you have against doubt.

Identifying the Issue

What can we learn from Thomas to apply in a crisis of faith? First we learn to identify the issue related to our doubt. What exactly do you feel is lacking? What exactly is keeping you from believing? What exactly is the problem? Be specific.

Thomas didn't feel like he could believe unless he had certain visual proof. Jesus tells him that he didn't need that proof at all. Almost everyone who has ever believed in the resurrection has done so without personally seeing Jesus and touching His scars! Jesus tells Thomas that faith does not require sight.

Neither does sight guarantee faith. People saw Jesus perform miracles and did not believe He was the Messiah. There are people who see video footage of the moon landing and yet refuse to believe man has ever been to the moon.

Nevertheless, when doubt erects a barrier to faith, it helps to identify the nature of the barrier. Identifying a problem is usually the first step toward a solution.

Thomas also teaches us the importance of community. Thomas doesn't keep his doubt a secret. He shares the issue with his friends. It would have done Thomas no good if he had known the issue related to his doubt but not communicated it to others.

Why do we keep our doubts secret? It usually boils down to pride. Maintaining a façade of impenetrable faith comes at the cost of faith. *Doubting* is not the adjective most of us want before our name. Thomas could have kept his mouth shut. We'd know him as Thomas "the Twin." Coming clean about doubt shatters the illusion that we have all the answers. The parent who knows it all. The pastor who has it figured out. The unwavering entrepreneur. These people don't exist. They are fictional characters of our fallen imagination, avatars we send into the world—into the church—in place of real Christians with real doubts.

Hidden doubt begets a cycle of doubt. Kids who grow up with fictional moms and dads who never question will not go to their parents with their own doubts. Why would they? How shameful for a high school student to admit her doubt to her spiritual supermom and superdad? We think that hiding doubt helps kids, but it has the opposite effect. A doubting teenager thinks that something must be wrong with them to be having questions, doubts, and uncertainty.

And then they go to college. Professors talk openly about questions pertaining to faith. Doubt is cathartic. Something hidden comes to light and the emotional and intellectual release is intoxicating. Finally, someone gives voice to doubt. Usually it's the beginning of the end. In the words of Joni Mitchell, God goes up the chimney.

Thomas doesn't keep his doubt a secret. He models something better. Something healthy. He tells other believers the nature of his struggle. He confesses his doubts.

Two things happen when doubt comes to light. Thomas gets help and the other disciples see how to handle doubt. Thomas becomes the object lesson: a moment of doubt in exchange for an eternity of discipleship.

Confessing doubt in the local church enables soul care. There are books to read. Verses to consider. Like 1 Corinthians 10:13, which says, "No temptation has overtaken you that is not common to man." The biblical model of discipleship, where older men disciple younger men and older women disciple younger women, provides a safe haven in which doubts can be voiced and resources can be shared.

If you are reading this book and dealing with doubt there are likely people in your church, or in your extended faith community, who have also wrestled with those particular doubts. Your crisis of faith can be shortened—or ended—by hearing the stories of how others have addressed their questions and by hearing the advice they received.

Sometimes the most spiritual thing you can do is invite an aged and thoughtful believer from church to lunch. Over lunch, share the question, experience, or burden that is causing your doubt. You will often find that they, or someone they know, have walked that road before.

You must be proactive about your own spiritual health in the same way you are about your physical health. No responsible person would ignore persistent or worsening physical problems without seeking medical help.

Spiritual heath is the same way. Festering doubts require help, and you must take the responsibility to seek that help. Your church leaders are a great place to start. But every believer has the Spirit. Every Christian is a priest. There is healing in the counsel and intercession of faithful saints committed to the authority of God's Word.

When Thomas confesses to others the nature of his doubt he is able to get help. That is an internal benefit. Keeping doubt a secret hurts you, and bringing it to light helps you.

But a crisis of faith isn't just about you. Doubt has both personal and communal implications. When doubt is brought out of the shadows and is confessed in community, others are encouraged. You are never the only person who struggles with doubt. You might be the only person who has the courage to admit your doubt. When you do, you encourage others to admit their doubt, get help, and make it through their crisis of faith.

Thomas wasn't the only disciple who doubted. More than one disciple doubted Jesus after His resurrection when He was with them on the mount of ascension (Matthew 28:16–20). The disciples doubted Jesus on the boat in the storm (Mark 4:35–41). Luke tells us Jesus appeared to His disciples after the resurrection. Jesus shows up and says to them, "Peace to you," before asking the disciples, "Why do doubts arise in your hearts?" (Luke 24:36–43).

What made Thomas unique was not his doubt. It was the fact he admitted his doubt. He brought his doubt to light. In doing so, he received mercy. He was able to see and touch the Savior, and Jesus used the occasion to encourage the disciples to believe by faith. They would not always have Jesus around to see and touch. Like John the Baptist, Thomas seeks Jesus.

Answers Take Time

One thing to remember in a crisis of faith is that answers don't always come immediately. Sometimes you have to wait. Thomas wasn't with the disciples the first time Jesus appeared. When the disciples told Thomas that they had seen the Lord, Thomas said, "Unless I see the nail marks in his hands and put my finger where the nails were, and put my hand into his side, I will not believe" (John 20:25 NIV).

Jesus doesn't show up that moment. He doesn't magically appear. Faith is not like ruby slippers in *The Wizard of Oz*; three heel clicks don't get you back home. After Thomas doubted and sought evidence, Scripture says, "A week later his disciples were in the house again, and Thomas was with them" (v. 26 NIV).

A week later!

That might not seem like much time, but in a crisis of faith, time moves slowly. An hour can seem like an eternity in a hospital room waiting to see a doctor. A minute on hold waiting for news about a loved one can seem like forever. In those prayer-filled moments of doubt and uncertainty, faith has to wait.

God is gracious and merciful in times of doubt, but He doesn't perform on our command. Consider this truth the next time you doubt. God may resolve the issue or provide an answer to the question that is leading to your doubt, but it might take some time. Waiting is an act of faith.

In order to make it through a crisis of faith, not only must you be willing to wait, but you must also be willing to wait in a certain way: worshipfully. Simply biding time will not automatically bolster faith.

Faith, hope, and love describe worshipful waiting. In a crisis of faith, there are things you do not know that cause a sense of instability. Nevertheless, there are backstops to faith. You know God exists. Even if you are angry at God, your anger is directed at something real. God's existence, love, sovereignty, and promises are backstops to faith when everything else is unknown and unclear.

Hope requires that you wait with a sense of expectation. Life has meaning and is going somewhere. Circumstances are not out of control, even when it seems that way. When your experiences appear to be in chaos, hope continues to believe in design and purpose.

Like many people, I grew up watching *The Joy of Painting* with Bob Ross. When there was nothing else on television, you could usually find Ross painting a seascape or creating "happy trees." When he started the painting, you could not tell what direction he was going. Slowly, during the course of the episode, the image in the mind of the painter emerged on the canvas. It was worth it to see blurred images and squiggly lines become trees, barns, waves, and other recognizable and beautiful images. If you tuned out you missed out.

Hope is clinging to the beauty of the image that has yet to emerge. When things are blurry and out of focus, waiting with hope is sticking around long enough to see a fraction of what God is doing, glimpses of His masterpiece.

Love believes all things (1 Corinthians 13:7). Waiting worshipfully is an act of defiance against unbelief. In the poem "Do not go gentle into that good night," Dylan Thomas writes, "Rage, rage against the dying of the light." Love is the rage of the life of faith against the death of unbelief. It is the will of the soul to exist and believe.

During my time as a hospice chaplain, on more than one occasion I witnessed the remarkable persistence of the human body against terminal illness. A person would breathe when you were sure they were done breathing. Eyes would open when they appeared to be closed for good. People sometimes live for days when they are given only hours, and weeks when given only days. Life wants to be lived.

Love keeps believing when circumstances pull all the plugs. Dogged and rugged belief, willful and persistent, determined and unrelenting. In order to make it through a crisis of faith you will need to wait worshipfully.

Tom Petty said it best: The waiting is the hardest part.

A crisis of faith is a test of endurance. Doubt wants to throw in the towel, but faith goes another round. Doubt tempts us with immediacy, but faith is patient. Questions come quick, but answers take time. Life can become chaotic with sudden unexpected circumstances, while order, structure, and purpose usually evolve slowly.

The Surprise of Not Wanting What You Thought You Needed

The story of Doubting Thomas has a surprise ending. All this time Thomas said he wanted to see and touch. Remember? That was the bargain. That was the demand. He had a simple condition of faith.

And then he waited. After a week Jesus shows up, and Thomas gets his wish. He can finally touch the scars and place his fingers on the marred hands. Then he will believe! Then it will all make sense! That was the deal.

But the Bible never says Thomas touched Jesus. He saw Jesus. He could have touched Jesus. John says the apostles touched Jesus. But after all that waiting, Scripture never says Thomas touched Jesus. On one hand, Scripture is silent on the issue. On the other hand, given the demand Thomas made to see *and touch*, any reference to touching Jesus by Thomas is conspicuously missing.

In literature this kind of device is called a cliffhanger. A cliffhanger makes a point by withholding easy resolution. The lesson of the story is built upon the tension of the narrative.

The story of Thomas has a happy ending. Thomas believes. In fact, he utters what is perhaps the clearest declaration of allegiance to Jesus in the Bible: "My Lord and my God!" (John 20:28). From Thomas we get one of the most direct and incontrovertible declarations of the deity of Jesus in all of Scripture. Out of a scene of great doubt comes a statement of great faith. Belief comes through a crisis stronger than before. That is how we want to make it through a crisis of faith.

But Thomas thought he needed to touch Jesus. And then he was able to touch Jesus. Others did touch Jesus. But on my reading of the story, Thomas didn't actually touch Jesus before his declaration of faith in Jesus, if ever. This is the point: Sometimes in a crisis of faith you do not need the evidence you think you need. You may find, like Thomas, the conditions of faith that seemed so important stop being so important over time. You learn how to keep believing in a difficult marriage. You make it through a hard season of parenting. You adjust to life with chronic pain.

God knows what we need. He knows how to preserve our faith. We make our demands and do our bargaining, and God is exceedingly gracious. When the crisis is over, things unfold in ways we never anticipated. We endure what we thought we could not endure, and we often do so without the answers we thought we needed.

Everyone has made the mistake of bargaining for signs from God as a sinful expression of doubt. We have all uttered demands as a condition of faith. "If You love me, God, then help me get this job." "God, if You really exist, then bring an end to this affliction." And when God has answered those prayers in a way that we like (i.e., we get the job or the affliction ends) it doesn't bring final closure to doubt. Doubt always has a new list of demands.

This is why Jesus says, "Blessed are those who have not seen and yet have believed" (John 20:29). We think that seeing something with our own eyes will resolve our doubts, but doubt is a problem of the heart, not the eyes. Thomas was sure he knew what he needed to believe, but he was wrong. He didn't need to touch. He didn't even need to see. He needed to believe the testimony of those God sent to deliver the message of the resurrection. Faith comes by hearing (Romans 10:17).

Bertrand Russell was a famous atheist in the twentieth century. He wrote an essay called "Why I Am Not a Christian" in which he argued that religions (such as Christianity) are not just untrue but dangerous. Russell's view that Christianity is bad for society has been called antitheism.

At some point later in his life, Russell was asked what he would say to God if he were to die and God did exist. Russell had an answer. "Not enough evidence, God. Not enough evidence."

There is never enough evidence for unbelief. Like all sin, the unbelieving heart is a bottomless pit. No amount of money can cure greed. No amount of food can cure gluttony. And no amount of evidence can cure unbelief.

No wonder the father with the demon-possessed son cried out, "I believe; help my unbelief!" (Mark 9:24). We need God to enable us to see the evidence. We do not need more evidence. We need God to open our closed eyes of unbelief. When God opens the eyes of unbelief, faith sees what has always been there.

In the beatitudes, Jesus says the pure in heart are blessed and will see God (Matthew 5:8). The pure in heart are believers who are made pure by the righteousness of Jesus and demonstrate new life through a pursuit of holiness.

When do they see God? When they die? Yes, but more than that: Believers see evidence of God in everything. From Charles Spurgeon's sermon on the Sermon on the Mount, he says:

> When his heart is clean, he will hear God's footfall everywhere in the garden of the earth in the cool of the day. He will hear God's voice in the tempest, sounding in peal on peal from the tops of the mountains. He will behold the Lord walking on the great and mighty waters, or see Him in every leaf that trembles in the breeze. Once get the heart right, and then God can be seen everywhere. To an impure heart, God cannot be seen

anywhere; but to a pure heart God is to be seen everywhere, in the deepest caverns of the sea, in the lonely desert, in every star that gems the brow of midnight!

Even with the whole universe as evidence, those not cleaned by the blood of Jesus will never see God. Evidence and arguments alone cannot give eyes to see. And those with greater faith see God more clearly. In the same sermon, Spurgeon continues:

> I think there are some Christians who never see God as well as others do—I mean some brethren who, from their peculiar constitution, seem naturally of a questioning spirit. They are generally puzzled about some doctrinal point or other, and their time is mostly taken up with answering objections and removing doubts. Perhaps some poor humble country woman who sits in the aisle, and who knows . . . nothing more than that her Bible is true, and that God always keeps His promises, sees a great deal more of God than the learned and quibbling brother who vexes himself about foolish questions to no profit.

Doubt Doesn't Define You

Thomas ended up with a nickname: Doubting Thomas. But the truth is, Peter had a much bigger moment of doubt. He denied Jesus three times! No one calls him Doubting Peter. Life is unfair.

The good news is that moments of doubt do not define you. In the same way Jesus praised John the Baptist for his courage even after he had doubted Jesus, so too Thomas went on to be a superhero in the history of evangelism and missions.

Based on reliable Christian tradition and the absence of evidence to the contrary, the consensus of scholars is that Thomas spread the gospel in India. It is believed he was martyred for Christ in the state of Chennai, where he is also buried. Thomas had wanted to touch the side of Jesus, where Jesus had been pierced with a spear. Ironically, the tradition is that Thomas was killed by a spear. Today you can visit the Tomb of Saint Thomas in Mylapore, India.

Fernando Ortega has the following line in a song titled "Shame" on his self-titled album, "Remember me. Not my shame. "

The good news for those who have trusted in Jesus is that God remembers us by the merit of Jesus and not by our shame. The shame of guilt, sin, and unbelief does not define us.

If doubt doesn't define us, then we also learn from Thomas that it doesn't control us. Thomas didn't spend the rest of his life sulking for the sake of his doubt. He had a life to live for Jesus. God had work for him to do. We shortchange the kingdom—and ourselves—when we let past failures keep us from present-day obedience.

Robin Williams starred as John Keating in the 1989 film *Dead Poets Society*. Keating is a high school English teacher who inspires a group of young men to find camaraderie and confidence through poetry, literature, and the arts. It is a great movie.

One line used in the film, which has since gained popularity, is the Latin phrase *carpe diem*, which means, "Seize the day." The phrase can be dated to Horace's *Odes*, written in the first century BC. In *Dead Poets Society*, Keating says "carpe diem" to motivate the young men in his class to do hard things and take control of their lives. He conveys the meaning of the phrase through the poem "To the Virgins, to Make Much of Time" by seventeenth-century poet Robert Herrick:

Gather ye rosebuds while ye may,

Old Time is still a-flying;

And this same flower that smiles today

Tomorrow will be dying.

Carpe diem as a philosophy is antithetical to Christianity. Its focus on the moment lacks the eternal perspective commanded in Scripture. The biblical idea of delayed reward and gratification runs contrary to *carpe diem*. The Bible teaches that union with Christ is the awaited treasure, which supports the virtues of patience, longsuffering, and temperance. The *carpe diem* ethos is expressed in the more recent acronym YOLO: you only live once.

For these reasons, the *carpe diem* philosophy often leads (not surprisingly) to broken relationships, disappointment, resentment, and anxiety. The fear of missing out is one fruit of *carpe diem*. It is impossible to be happy seizing the day when the Bible says your life is a vapor, grass that withers, and a flower that fades.

And yet, if the past does not define us, and if the future is wide open to those who turn from sin to follow Jesus, then there is a sense in which as Christians we follow Christ away from past failures into a preferred future of faith, hope, and love. *Carpe diem*, in this sense, is being free to choose faith over doubt.

I am sure that at some point Thomas had other doubts. We all do. But his life as a faithful disciple, missionary, preacher, and evangelist led him to take the gospel where it had never gone.

What do we learn from Thomas? In a crisis of faith, you make it through by confessing doubt, seeking help, finding answers, trusting the testimony of Scripture, resisting the temptation to bargain, and remembering that doubt doesn't define you.

Chapter 4

Peter: To Whom Else Shall We Go?

*I*n the book *Pilgrim's Progress,* the main character (Christian) must stay on the path to the Celestial City. Along the way, there are other paths going off in different directions, which Christian must avoid. The other paths are attractive because the road to the Celestial City is difficult.

Jesus said few enter the narrow gate that leads to eternal life, but many enter the broad gate that leads to destruction (Matthew 7:13–14). Every person must choose the gate they will enter and the path they will take. The choice is made once at the point of salvation, an event the Bible calls being born again (John 3:3). Salvation is permanent and irrevocable (Philippians 1:6).

However, people who have been saved must also make the decision to follow Jesus on a daily basis. Deciding to turn away from sin and follow Jesus is called repentance. Over time, Christians who practice repentance grow in holiness, a process the Bible calls sanctification (1 Thessalonians 4:3). Sanctification is a slow-motion miracle.[1] It is God's patient work in believers, graciously accomplished by His Spirit, through the power of His Word, in the nurturing community of His people.

---

[1] I am indebted here to Milton Vincent, as heard at the 2019 California State Baptist Convention Pastor's Conference speaker roundtable at Shadow Mountain Community Church in El Cajon, California.

Martin Luther's first thesis in the famous list of ninety-five theses says that Jesus willed the entire life of a believer to be one of repentance. Christians make the initial choice to follow Christ and the daily choice to continue on His path. The grace that saves us is also the grace that enables us to persevere. God's grace always demands a response. In *Mere Christianity*, C. S. Lewis says that Jesus must be the Lord, a madman, or the devil of hell, and each of us must choose. In *Pensées*, Blaise Pascal likened belief in God to a bet that each of us must make; to believe or not to believe, that is the question.

An increasing number of people identify as agnostic, a person who does not know whether or not to believe in God. In reality, Paul says in Romans 1:21 that people know there is a God but do not want to worship Him as God. The problem is not primarily intellectual but spiritual. Agnostics think they have avoided the choice between theism (belief in God) and atheism (belief in no God) and are spiritually neutral.

But there is no spiritual neutrality. Jesus says each person is either with Him or against Him (Matthew 12:30). Everyone has placed a bet, entered a gate, and is on a path. In a crisis of faith, you wonder whether or not you have chosen well.

Types of Doubt

Not every crisis of faith is the same. John the Baptist had a crisis of faith because he was in prison. His unbelief had to do with his experience of evil and suffering. Thomas, on the other hand, had a different kind of doubt. He doubted because he couldn't comprehend the idea that Jesus was physically alive after being dead for three days.

In general, there are three kinds of doubt: experiential, intellectual, and emotional. Experiential doubt arises from trials, hardships, evil, and suffering. For instance, a Christian who goes through a serious illness may doubt whether God is for them (Roman 8:28–29). Or a Christian parent who sees their child bullied and has exhausted their options in regard to protecting their child may doubt that God cares. Doubt that arises when life is particularly hard may be experiential doubt.

Intellectual doubt, on the other hand, induces a crisis of faith that is primarily related to some vexing question or objection to belief. High school and college students often go through a period of intellectual doubt related to challenges to the Christian worldview from curriculum or teachers. If your crisis of faith started with a hard teaching in Scripture or something you read or heard that seemed to undermine the truth of the Bible, then you are most likely suffering from intellectual doubt. A person who questions their faith because of an unresolved question may be experiencing intellectual doubt.

Emotional doubt is unbelief associated with mental and emotional states such as anxiety, depression, or despair. These states can be brought on by intellectual or experiential circumstances, but they can also occur by themselves, unrelated to any known cause. A person who questions their faith because of how they feel may be experiencing emotional doubt.

Experiential, intellectual, and emotional doubt often go together and are usually intertwined. A health crisis may trigger experiential doubt, which leads to emotional doubt. Pain often leads to despair. Emotional doubt can increase susceptibility to intellectual doubt. Despair often leads to confusion. These types of doubt can be separate and are unique but can also overlap, merge, and combine.

Whatever the kind of doubt, all kinds of doubt are sinful. Hebrews 3:12 says, "Take care, brothers, lest there be in any of you an evil, unbelieving heart, leading you to fall away from the living God." Unbelief is evil.

Sin is both breaking God's commands and failing to reflect His character. We are image bearers of God. That is both a privilege and a responsibility. We break the first commandment when we put ourselves above God and His Word: We play god over God. As John Stott says in his book *The Cross of Christ,* "The essence of sin is man substituting himself for God."

Adam and Eve were the first humans and also the first doubters. God graciously gave Adam and Eve every tree in the Garden of Eden to enjoy—except one. Satan planted the seed of unbelief when he asked Eve, "Did God actually say, 'You shall not eat of any tree in the garden'?" (Genesis 3:1). Satan isn't seeking clarification in order to better understand and obey God. His question is a subversive tactic intended to induce doubt and foment rebellion. It worked then, and it works now. Eve ate, and then Adam, and humanity was plunged into an ongoing war with sin and death.

The twentieth-century American author Flannery O'Connor was a master at what has been called a Southern-gothic style of writing. This means her stories were dark, pointed, and shocking. Yet in the darkness of her stories Flannery O'Connor wove themes of grace and redemption. Take for example "A Good Man Is Hard to Find." In it, a criminal called "the Misfit" points a gun at an old lady in a fancy hat. The old lady looks the part of a righteous and upstanding person. In the scene, you'd think she is the "good guy" if not for O'Connor pulling back the curtain on the woman's deep-seated self-righteousness and hypocrisy. In one pivotal scene shortly before the woman is shot, the Misfit and the woman discuss whether or not Jesus rose from the dead, and the woman realizes she and the Misfit are really not so different:

> "I wasn't there so I can't say He didn't," the Misfit said. "I wisht I had of been there," he said, hitting the ground with his fist. "It ain't right I wasn't there because if I had of been there I would of known. Listen lady," he said in a high voice, "if I had of been there I would of known and I wouldn't be like I am now." His voice seemed about to crack and the grandmother's head cleared for an instant. She saw the man's face twisted close to her own as if he were going to cry and she murmured, "Why you're one of my babies. You're one of my own children!" She reached out and touched him on the shoulder. The Misfit sprang back as if a snake had bitten him and shot her three times through the chest. Then he put his gun down on the ground and took off his glasses and began to clean them.

In this story, the woman saw an unexpected family resemblance in the Misfit. The two are not as different as they initially appeared. Both are deeply flawed sinners capable of great evil.

Theologians describe the moment that Adam and Eve ate the fruit, when sin entered the world, as the fall. Ever since the fall, the world has been cursed. Doubt is part of the curse. Humanity follows Adam and Even in questioning God as a subversive act to justify sinful desires. We are a misfit race. We blame God for our own unbelief as though God has failed. In fact, we are the ones committing the crimes and digging our own graves.

Doubt runs in the family.

The good news is we have a brother—one man in the whole lineage of humanity—who didn't doubt, falter, or sin. He obeyed the Father perfectly, and then gave Himself as a sacrifice to redeem rebels and pay the penalty for the treachery of His brothers and sisters.

The Curse of Doubt and the Hope of Heaven

Remember the curse? Sin brought a curse upon all creation. Jesus *became* the curse (Galatians 3:13). Jesus is the one and only truly good man, and He is able to make us good again. This is why at Christmastime Christians sing Isaac Watt's classic hymn, "Joy to the World":

No more let sins and sorrows grow,
Nor thorns infest the ground;
He comes to make His blessings flow
Far as the curse is found,
Far as the curse is found,
Far as, far as the curse is found

After sin entered the world, God promised to send a Savior who would defeat sin and death (Genesis 3:15). The promised Savior would be born from the seed of woman, a veiled reference to the virgin birth of Jesus. It is Jesus who undoes the curse.

What does this mean for doubt? It means we will not always struggle with unbelief. There is a day coming when doubt—like grief and cancer and injustice—will cease. When you think about the eternal state, and union with Christ, think about how wonderful it will be to have complete trust in God.

When you trust, you rest. An airplane flying at night will have sleeping passengers if they trust things are going well. Usually this means a smooth flight! Add some moderate-to-severe turbulence, and no one is sleeping! Why? You simply cannot rest when you do not trust that the pilots have things under control.

In a crisis of faith, it can be hard to sleep. You wake up in the night worried about whether or not God will provide, or what will happen in your situation, or with the person you love. Eventually physical exhaustion (or medication) kicks in, and you fall back asleep. But what we want is peaceful rest: trust that God has things in control. We want peace in the storms. Ultimately, we want the storms to end.

It helps to remember that in the grand narrative of redemption, heaven is the place where faith is perfected and all doubts cease. In the absence of doubt we will enjoy perfect peace. No more worry. No more doubt. Right now we enjoy the Sabbath, or rest, from our works of righteousness. We rest in Jesus, who is our salvation. This is a glimpse of the rest we will enjoy when all our life is made perfect in His presence.

All doubt is evidence of the curse, but not all doubt is the same. The work of Jesus undoes the curse, but we will not enjoy the full benefits of His work until we are reunited with Him. In the meantime, Peter has something to teach us about making it through a crisis of faith.

Jesus Empties the Room

In the Gospel of John, there is a story about Peter. If Thomas deserves to be called Doubting Thomas then Peter has an earned doctorate in doubt. Peter denies Jesus three times, and then after Jesus ascends back to heaven, Peter appears to align himself with a group of people demanding that Gentile converts obey Old Covenant commands. Peter continues to struggle with doubt.

In John 6 we learn a lesson from Peter about withstanding doubt. Jesus has just fed the five thousand, and the multitudes are following Him. In terms of optics, His ministry is looking great. But Jesus knows that many people are following Him for a free meal and a miracle.

For this reason, Jesus begins to use the bread He provided as an object lesson. He reminds the audience of the manna God provided from heaven to save Israel. In the same way, Jesus Himself has come from heaven to save God's people. Jesus must be consumed by faith (John 6:40).

The crowds do not like this message. They want the bread and the wine but not the body and the blood. They want a king without laws: deliverance without the Cross. In short, they don't want Jesus.

Jesus wasn't fooled, and He didn't panic. He intended to touch a nerve. Jesus separated the genuine followers from the fair-weather masses. The people who left seem to have forgotten about the prophesies from the Old Testament about a Savior born miraculously of a woman in Bethlehem. The people who left didn't seem to think Jesus could have been the Messiah come from heaven: "Is not this Jesus, the son of Joseph, whose father and mother we know?" (v. 42).

It says many of His disciples (those who had been following Him) heard the teaching of Jesus and said, "This is a hard saying; who can listen to it?" (v. 60). Picture a large church filled with people, and as the preacher gives the sermon, the room empties, leaving only a handful of people sitting in the pews. This is the picture that John paints of the masses leaving Jesus over His difficult teaching. John tells us, "Many of his disciples turned back and no longer walked with him" (v. 66).

Take a moment to consider the implications of the story so far. First, Jesus taught things that were hard to hear. Second, these hard teachings drove casual followers away. Third, Jesus knows this will happen and doesn't change His message.

A crisis of faith can be brought on by a hard teaching. If you've been raised in a church that avoids hard teachings in order to accommodate the casual masses, then at some point, Jesus is going to rub you the wrong way. Casual disciples want the bread and the wine but not the body and the blood. There are churches whose entire ministry methodology is to attract and keep casual disciples. To do this, you simply need to avoid the hard teachings of Jesus.

But there is a hook beneath the bait. Jesus knows His words draw a line in the sand. God's Word is life to the living and death to the dying. It is a stumbling block of offense (vv. 61–65). The Father has to grant eyes to see and ears to hear (v. 65).

The Most Important Question in Scripture

Jesus turns to the twelve and asks a simple and life-changing question, "Do you want to go away as well?" (v. 67). In this moment Jesus shows Himself to be unlike any sinful human teacher. If you have ever done any teaching or public speaking, it is a terrifying thing to be in front of a room full of people (let alone a large room full of people) and have the impression that whatever you're saying is not being well received. In that moment, your impulse is to do whatever you can to regain attention, recapture interest, and reanimate your teaching.

At one trade conference I attended, a breakout session was packed with about five hundred attendees. The speaker began, and it got off to a rocky start. A few people trickled out. Ten minutes into the presentation, and the speaker was having technical issues, and more people began to leave. He tried to make jokes and was visibly uncomfortable. I have never seen a public speaker so completely lose his audience, but he tried everything. By the end of the session, there were less than twenty people remaining; it was brutal.

But Jesus isn't panicked. He doesn't pander. This is all happening according to plan.

Pivotal moments in the Bible are often punctuated with great questions. I would list among those top questions the following: "Did God actually say, 'You shall not eat of any tree in the garden'?" (Genesis 3:1), "Teacher, what must I do to inherit eternal life?" (Luke 18:18), "Who do you say that I am?" (Matthew 16:15), and "Where shall I go from your Spirit? Or where shall I flee from your presence?" (Psalm 139:7).

Yet here in John 6 is what is arguably the best question for making it through a crisis of faith. It is found in verse 68, and it is Simon Peter's response to Jesus. Remember that Jesus asked, "Do you want to go away as well?" and Peter responds with a question of his own: "To whom shall we go?"

In a crisis of faith, Jesus offends you. He says something you don't like. He doesn't show up the way you want. He puts you somewhere you don't want to be. He calls you to give something up you enjoy. He takes something from you. At some point, Jesus makes you mad, and you take offense at Him.

In that moment—in a crisis of faith—you stand up and head for the door. Doubt is always packing our bags. Showing us the exit. Promising greener grass elsewhere.

But before you walk away, seriously consider Peter's question. Where are you going to go? It is an undeniable fact that whenever you leave somewhere or someone you have to go to something else or to someone else. Jesus asks, "Do you want to go?" and Peter asks in return, "To whom?" Jesus is telling Peter to seriously consider the alternatives.

And so, when you are tempted to walk away from Jesus, seriously consider the alternatives. I will grant that Jesus says some hard things. He has rules. He is willing to be your Savior, but He insists on also being your Lord. As Dietrich Bonhoeffer says in his book *The Cost of Discipleship*, grace is free, but it is costly.

If you find yourself walking away from Jesus, you are always walking toward something (or someone) else. If you reject the teaching of

Jesus, the rule of Jesus, then who is going to replace Him? You cannot just dethrone Jesus from your heart. Someone will take His place.

Consider the Alternatives

Peter says to Jesus, "Lord, to whom shall we go? You have the words of eternal life, and we have believed, and have come to know, that you are the Holy One of God" (John 6:68–69). If you, or someone you know, is tempted to abandon the faith, it is always a challenge to know how to respond. On the basis of this passage, consider the following response: "Okay, where are we going?"

Leaving is easy; going somewhere is harder. Why did you come to Jesus in the first place? You needed a creator to explain your existence. You need a savior to rescue you from sin, guilt, and shame. You need a purpose to give your life meaning. You need something after death to give you hope and purpose. If you reject Jesus, do you think you'll find someone else who can provide those things?

Consider the alternatives.

No other religion is more intellectually fulfilling, historically reliable, and socially beneficial. No other person in the history of humanity other than Jesus could credibly claim to be the Savior of the world. No one else but Jesus predicted they would rise from the dead and then followed through on their promise. No other book has changed the world (for the better) more than the Bible. Simply put, Christianity is not just another religion. It is the only religion that makes sense of our past and our problems and offers a historical solution and future hope.

Giving up Christianity is the wrong move. You stand to lose infinitely more than you stand to gain. You lose a coherent explanation of sin and a savior, and you gain a new set of harder problems. Having rejected the biblical story of evil, you still struggle with evil, only now you don't know why it is evil. You still deal with hypocritical people, for instance, but without Christ there is no compelling reason to be kind, loving, or gracious to hypocrites; nor is there any compelling reason to expect this from others when you act hypocritically.

Saying no to something means saying yes to something else. Think about what you will eat for your next meal. If you are at someone's house and they ask you, "Do you want a hamburger?" and you say no you have effectively eliminated one option. Imagine your host responds, "All right, that leaves us with meatloaf or salmon."

Unfortunately, imagine that while you may not be excited at the moment about a hamburger, you absolutely hate meatloaf and salmon. When you originally said no to the hamburger, you did not realize that there were only a few options. You need to eat and cannot go hungry. Realizing you passed up the best option unintentionally, you tell your host you'll be happy with the hamburger.

Homo Religiosus

When it comes to religion, humans must choose. Humans worship by nature just as surely as dogs bark and lions roar. Worship is human nature.

Mircea Eliade was a twentieth-century Romanian historian of religion and professor at the University of Chicago. In his book *The Sacred and the Profane: The Nature of Religion* he argues that across cultures, humans have a concept of the sacred, practices to observe the sacred, and anxiety associated with rejection of the sacred. Eliade borrows from German religious scholar Rudolf Otto in his 1917 book *Das Heilige* (the sacred) where Otto talks about the sacred as that which is beyond the natural realm and installs in us a sense of wonder and mystery. The sacred is not an abstract concept. It is that which determines what we value and how we choose to live.

Eliade takes Otto's concept of the sacred and looks cross-culturally at humanity and concludes that humans are religious by nature. We are not merely *homo sapiens* (meaning wise man), we are homo religiosus (meaning religious man). On the evolutionary model of humanity, humanity has evolved as a *genus (homo)* from *erectus* (standing up) to *habilus* (working) to *sapien* (wisdom), which includes worship. Even from a secular academic perspective, full humanity, on an evolutionary scale, involves worship.

The Bible cannot support a Darwinian model of evolution. On that model, the universe is the product of random mutation and natural selection. These concepts are incompatible with the sovereignty and foreknowledge of God, that God controls the universe and everything unfolds according to His design and plan. Eliade may be wrong about evolution, but he is right about worship.

Solomon says in Ecclesiastes 3:11, "[God] has put eternity into man's heart." The prophet Isaiah says God made humans to declare God's praise (Isaiah 43:21). Worship reflects the image of God in every person (Genesis 1:27). Jesus says the job of humanity is to love God and each other (Luke 10:27).

There is strong biblical and sociological evidence that worship is natural. This is obvious by looking at global statistics on religion and belief in God. Globally, eight out of ten people self-identify as religious.[2] Nine out of ten people (globally) believe in God.

By way of analogy, consider the global statistics on color-sighted-ness (people who see the normal range of colors). One out of twelve men are colorblind (and one out of every two hundred women).

We understand that the ability to see color is normal, and the inability to see color is a deficiency or indication of visual impairment. In the same way, belief in God is the proper response to the world in which we live. Failure to see the evidence for God's existence reflects a spiritual deficiency and moral impairment that results from sin.

Long before Otto or Eliade, John Calvin made the analogy between physical sight and the ability to spiritually apprehend the existence of God. In his book *Institutes of the Christian Religion*, Calvin says, "There is within the human mind, and indeed by natural instinct, an awareness of divinity." Calvin calls this the "*sensus divinitatus*," sense of the divine. God designed humans with physical senses to know the physical world and a divine sense to know He exists.

The Apostle Paul talks about this in Romans 1, where he says belief in God is made evident by nature and God's divine attributes so that humankind is without excuse for unbelief. Paul says the human problem is not that we do not know God exists, the problem is that we do not want to accept the implications of God's existence, namely, that He would get to tell us how to live (vv. 18–23).

In a crisis of faith, where a person is tempted to disbelieve in God, he or she is struggling against his or her own nature. It is more than a crisis of faith; it is a crisis of being and essence. A crisis of faith is normal, but it is far more serious than we first imagined. What is at stake

---

[2] Pew Research Center, "The Global Religious Landscape," December 18, 2012, https://www.pewforum.org/2012/12/18/global-religious-landscape-exec/.

is not merely where one goes when one dies, it is the very question, "What am I?" A crisis of faith is an existential crisis. To deny God fundamentally alters what it means to be human.

The whole universe is designed for man to worship. God says in Genesis 1:14, "Let there be lights in the expanse of the heavens to separate the day from the night. And let them be for signs and seasons, and for days and years. " The Hebrew word for *seasons* (*moed*) in the English Standard Version is footnoted to mean "appointed times." Throughout the Old Testament, this common word refers to appointed times and places of worship. God establishes the sun and moon to direct human beings in worship. Human beings are made to worship, and the universe is ordered to facilitate worship.

All this to say that worship is serious business. The New Testament says Jesus came at just the right time (Galatians 4:4–5) and will return at just the right time (Hebrews 10:37). Next time you look at the sun or other stars or the moon in the night sky remember that everything is made for worship, including you.

The Wisdom of Belief

When Peter asks, "To whom shall we go?" he is stating a human dilemma. Humans must worship, but a system of worship (religion) must answer at least five basic questions: (1) Where do we come from? (2) What went wrong? (3) What can be done to fix it? (4) How should we live? (5) Where are we going?

Peter is not merely making a point about his own limitations or the limitations of the remaining disciples. Peter is speaking for all of us; there is nowhere else to go for eternal life. Salvation is only found in Jesus.

Meaning is also only found in Jesus. He is the only one who can make sense of our humanity—where we come from, what went wrong, what can be done to fix it, how we should live, and where we are going.

The whole of human history and meaning is bound in the person and work of Jesus. If we lose Jesus, then we lose everything. Jesus doesn't just save our souls, He saves and restores our humanity. The world apart from Jesus doesn't make sense. The self apart from Jesus doesn't make sense. Jesus is the interpretive key to both self-understanding and our understanding of the universe.

It makes sense to believe (and to keep believing) in Jesus. Given that we are religious by nature, not worshipping is not an option. As Blaise Pascal observes in his book *Pensées*, Christianity explains both the greatness and wretchedness of man. The greatness of humanity comes from being made in God's image. The wretchedness of man comes from our sinful rebellion against God. We are the problem, not the solution.

God is the solution. God the Son becomes a human to do what humans cannot and will not do: fulfill the law, defeat sin and death, and ascend into heaven. Jesus is the first human to escape sin and death (1 Corinthians 15:20). His promise, and the hope of salvation, is that He plans to take us with Him if we believe.

Considering the alternatives may include exploring other religions. Contrary to popular opinion, world religions do not all teach the same thing. Reading credible sources that explain what other religions teach may help you see and appreciate the truth and beauty of the Bible.

For instance, Islam teaches that Jesus is a good prophet but that He didn't die for our sins. Of course Jesus cannot be a good prophet, even by the lights of Islam. Jesus *prophesied* his own death and resurrection. If Jesus didn't die and rise again then He is absolutely not a good prophet! Islam has no sin-bearing savior, no assurance of salvation, no unconditional love or unearned grace. Because Islam teaches that Paradise was not on earth, there is no future hope of redemption for creation to support the inherent value of the material world.

The four noble truths of Buddhism are right to identify the problem of suffering, but at every point, Buddhism gets it wrong about suffering. Buddhism teaches that all life is suffering. But life is not all suffering. Moments of tender love, compassion, justice, and beauty are not suffering. If everything is suffering, then nothing is suffering. In saying that everything is suffering, Buddhism negates the reality of suffering to an illusion. Because suffering is an illusion, the key to happiness is transcending this world through mindfulness and meditation, with the ultimate hope of enlightenment, the dissolution of self, and escape from the suffering associated with rebirth and death (*samsara*). Nirvana is not a place but a state in which suffering ceases, but so too does the self. All good stories have a beginning and an end; Buddhism lacks both.

A cursory look at two world religions shows glaring deficiencies. Other religions also lack what only Christianity can provide: answers to the five questions every human by nature asks themselves.

World religions such as Islam, Buddhism, and Hinduism simply cannot provide meaningful answers and therefore cannot make sense of human existence. The result is that where these religions thrive, human life, and life itself, has lost meaning. The absence of meaning is called nihilism. Peter says to Jesus, "You have the words of eternal life" (John 6:68).

In other words, there is nowhere else to go to find the answers that only Jesus can provide. No other savior is able to take sin and conquer death. No other religion can explain the greatness and wretchedness of the human family.

The Japanese poet and Buddhist monk Kobayashi Issa once wrote:

This world of dew—
Is only the world of dew—
And yet . . . oh and yet . . .

The backstory to the poem is recorded in the book *The Spring of My Life and Selected Haiku: Kobayashi Issa*, a collection of Issa's work translated by Sam Hamil, who wrote a summary of Issa's life in the book. After his father died, Issa struggled to secure his inheritance. Issa experienced loss after loss as his children died at young ages and then he lost his wife. The impermanence of life and the Buddhist worldview of the illusion of suffering is evident in the poem; *the world is dew*.

Notice, however, the final line of the poem, "And yet . . . oh and yet." The author knows his experience of life does not match with his Buddhist philosophy. Suffering is painful because life is real. The passing of the physical world is contrasted with the impulsive desire for eternity: God made us to long for eternity. Stories about vampires and fountains of youth are all variations on humanity's unshakable obsession with eternal life.

We want to hold on to the things that are passing, and to the people who have passed. There is nothing in Buddhism that can provide a personal eternity in the presence of a personal God and the hope that we will be reunited with those who have died. Buddhism, like all religions other than Christianity, simply cannot provide for the deepest yearnings of the soul; *and yet . . . oh and yet.* The author knows what we know: There is more to life than meets the eye.

The Paradox of Choice

A person tempted to leave Jesus should consider the alternatives. People don't usually dream about running away from home to live on the streets. As was noted in the first chapter, leaving is easy; finding somewhere to go is hard.

Imagine you give into doubt and deny Jesus. This will not improve your life in any meaningful or lasting way.

It is not possible for the regenerate believer—the person who has been born again—to lose their faith. In John 10:28 Jesus emphatically says He will not lose a single one of the sheep (i.e., those who have come to Jesus by faith). In Romans 8:30 Paul says all those whom God chose (i.e., those who have come to Jesus by faith) will be glorified (i.e., they will all make it to heaven). In Ephesians 1:13–14 Paul says the Spirit is given to believers as a deposit guaranteeing our inheritance. In the end, saving faith always wins.

Nevertheless, in a time of crisis of faith, it is helpful to seriously consider the alternatives. Consider what you would lose if you were to lose Jesus. When you lack appreciation for something (or someone), a short scare in losing that thing (or person) has the immediate effect of inducing gratitude. In a crisis of faith, we tend to take our faith (what little we may have at the moment) for granted. Imagining it lost altogether is sobering and has two immediate results. First, we realize what psychologists call the paradox of choice, and second, we confront the necessity of worship.

Jean-Paul Sartre famously said that man is condemned to be free because "once thrown into the world, he is responsible for everything he does." In modern society, people are accustomed to blaming everything on something (or someone) else. The Freudian excuse is to blame upbringing for bad choices. The genetic excuse is to blame biological makeup for bad choices. The Marxist excuse is to blame oppression from other groups for bad choices. The Christian version of this excuse is to blame Satan or bad churches for bad decisions.

Sartre had been a prisoner of war in Nazi Germany. He observed firsthand the atrocities the Nazi soldiers committed and then blamed on "following orders." Sartre found that despite the physical constraints of prison, he was free in regard to thought and belief.

In regard to religious belief, Sartre was an accomplished atheist. In the vein of Nietzsche, he believed that God was dead and that rather than hearing from God, we are permitted to "touch only his corpse." Sartre resisted the gravitational pull of nihilism, however, insisting that life had meaning in so far as we make free choices. Any choice guided by such things as tradition or social expectations was labeled *bad faith*, a term Sartre and his partner Simone de Beauvoir used to describe lacking the courage to own up to one's freedom.

I agree that we are responsible for our choices, and that influence does not determine our destiny, nor do genetics. The soul is largely responsible for the body, and, essentially, a human is a soul that will never die. Where Sartre goes wrong (there are many places, but in this regard) pertains to his views of the self.

Sartre understood that most people develop a sense of self based upon other people's views about themselves. Sartre himself was brilliant, but early on in life, he developed a self-identity plagued by insecurities over his short stature and eyes that pointed in different directions.

It is, of course, easy to understand that everyone is influenced by the perceptions of others. Most people never escape the opinions of others in regard to their own self-understanding. Perhaps people who are regarded as "great" have an elevated internal sense of self. But people whose internal sense of self is greater—or even just different—than popular opinion are regarded as narcissistic or even delusional.

In Christian circles, there is much talk about finding self-identity in Christ. This sounds good, and is certainly better than finding self-identity from the opinions of others or dreaming it up within yourself, but usually the Christian version of self-identity is thinly veiled Rogerian self-esteem.[3] It is the theological equivalent of *Saturday Night Live's* character Stuart Smalley, played by Al Franken, who stared into a mirror and declared, "I'm good enough, I'm smart enough, and and doggone it, people like me."

---

[3] Carl Rogers is a famous American psychologist and a founder of the modern self-esteem movement.

People spend a lot of time trying to construct the self. Reading books, listening to podcasts, deep breathing, personality tests—it's big business. Personality tests alone are a multibillion-dollar industry. Despite no conclusive scientific evidence that personality tests are any more reliable than horoscopes, Christians follow the business world in thinking that answering random questions will magically hold the key to self-understanding.

Where adults buy identity through personality tests, teenagers pay for identity in revolving styles that they try on in search of themselves. The phases we all go through are like dress rehearsals for life. Like one individual playing all the characters in a John Hughes film, we go through stages—the jock, the brain, the artist, the rebel, the beauty, etc.

Christian theology offers something that saves the time, money, frustration, and embarrassment of the modern construction of the self. God defines the self. It is not a mystery to be discovered or a test to be taken.

The self is revealed by God. Each human is both an image bearer and a depraved rebel. Through faith in Christ alone the image is restored and the rebel-self is restored to sonship (Galatians 3:26). God's children are transformed to be more like Jesus, a process (called sanctification) about the direction of your life, not the perfection of your life.

God's children wrestle against sinful desires on a daily basis. Desires that go against God's Word are inherently sinful. Becoming a Christian does not mean that all sinful desires go away immediately. With time and maturity many sinful desires are replaced by holy desires. Some sinful desires, however, will be a lifelong struggle of self-denial and self-control. For this reason, the Bible says, "Abstain from the passions of the flesh" (1 Peter 2:11).

Christians are simultaneously both sinner and saint. We are called to live out the holy desires of our new identity in Christ and not the sinful desires of our old identity apart from Christ (Romans 6:6–23). The inner turmoil of dying to self is exhausting, and failure is discouraging. In a crisis of faith, it can appear easier to give in to our sinful desires and to let them define us.

The attraction of giving up (and giving in) can often be perceived as the opportunity to create oneself—to be free of God's rules and laws and decide whom we want to be *apart* from God. But if Sartre is right, then freedom without God is a kind of condemnation. God's laws are good. They free us from the existential crisis of having to choose what we are and what we want to be.

Meanwhile the paradox of choices says too many choices lead to inaction, debilitating anxiety, and depression. There is no greater example of the depression related to choice than in regard to the burden of creating the self, day after day after day.

What is at stake if you walk away from God? You lose God, to be sure. But in a crisis of faith, you're not sure that is a loss. That is why it is a crisis of faith!

You may not be sure that God exists, but you know you exist. You undoubtedly care about yourself. Your identity and value are connected to God, in whose image you are made. A crisis of faith is inevitably also a crisis of self. If God is lost, then so too is human worth.

As Peter asks: To whom shall we go?

Words that Keep You from Leaving

The answer Peter gives to Jesus reveals something else that is tremendously helpful to surviving a crisis of faith. Peter follows up his question ("To whom shall we go?") with a statement: "You have the words of eternal life, and we have believed, and have come to know, that you are the Holy One of God" (John 6:68–69).

We come to God through His Word, and we stay with God by His Word. The Word of God—by which I mean the Bible—is the glue used by the Spirit to bind us to the Son in fellowship with the Father. The triune God uses His Word to get us through a crisis of faith.

God has preserved His Word. When apologists talk about the manuscript evidence for the New Testament (more than eight thousand ancient Greek manuscripts alone dating to the second century), they are showing evidence for what the Bible claims about itself: The word of God will never pass away. (See Isaiah 40:6–8; Matthew 24:35; and 1 Peter 1:25).

It is good to know that God preserves the Bible. However, Christians often forget that the Bible preserves us. By the power of the Spirit, over the centuries, the church has preserved the Bible, and the Bible has preserved the church.

In a crisis of faith, we look for ways to reinvigorate faith. We try a new church, read the latest book, check out new worship music, or attend a new conference. These things can be helpful. They are not bad in and of themselves. However, they are not substitutes for the Word. To the extent that they communicate the truths of Scripture, newly introduced books and other resources can be life-giving. The *source* of that life, however, is the Word of God. Make sure you are regularly going to the source.

Jesus says we live by His Word (Matthew 4:4). The psalmist declares multiple times in Psalm 119 that the Word of God revives the heart: Something like CPR for the soul.

In the Book of Joshua, Israel is commanded to trust God and live faithfully in the land. The book centers on the example of a man named Caleb who models the kind of faithfulness God commands. Caleb is one of the two spies in the Book of Numbers who returns from his mission with a report favoring obedience to God, while the other twelve report in such a way as to discourage faithful obedience (Numbers 13:17–33). Caleb waits forty-five years before he receives the reward for his faithfulness, and this is described in the Book of Joshua (Joshua 14:1–15). Imagine waiting patiently for forty-five years to receive a reward for something you did when you were young.

It is tempting to dismiss Caleb as having some kind of unique ability to believe, something like Michael Jordan's unique ability to jump. In thinking this way, we attempt to relieve ourselves of expecting we would ever exhibit Caleb's wholehearted faith and dismiss our failures under the guise of being "normal Christians." But the text of the Bible does not allow for this exemption. Caleb is not held forth as having Jordan-like spirituality. Rather, he simply believes what God has said. Multiple times in the story, Caleb refers to what God has said.

Caleb survives being alone and oppressed by clinging to what God had promised. So it is with Christians who survive a crisis of faith: They refuse to forget what God has said. His Word becomes daily food. In the middle of uncertainty and insecurity, the enduring Word preserves the soul. In *The Greatest Fight in the World*, Spurgeon says, "The

Word of God is quite sufficient to interest and bless the souls of men throughout all time; but novelties soon fail."

Fighting a crisis of faith with Christian novelties is doomed to fail. The Word—alone—is the sword capable of slaying unbelief. Peter doesn't leave Jesus. He makes it through his times of doubt just as all true disciples make it through their times of doubt. Jesus has eternal life. His Word gives us life and keeps us living. Apart from Jesus there is no meaning or purpose. If we lose Jesus we lose ourselves. Life with Jesus may be scary at times, but life apart from Jesus is unbearably terrifying.

Regardless of the type of doubt you experience, allow yourself to consider the alternatives. If you leave Jesus, where else will you go? There are no better alternatives. You will worship something, and anything you worship other than Jesus will leave you empty. Without Jesus, the past is a mystery, the self is a stranger, the future is uncertain, and forgiveness is impossible. Without Jesus you have more problems and fewer solutions. As bad as things get in a crisis of faith, they are worse without Jesus.

Chapter 5

Elijah: The Spiritual and Physical Aspects of Doubt

Perhaps no single story in the Old Testament better illustrates what a crisis of faith looks like, and how to make it through a crisis of faith, than the story of the prophet Elijah. The books of 1 and 2 Kings were written to Israel while they were in captivity. They answer questions a captive people would have asked, such as "Is God real?" "Does God keep His promises?" "Should I keep following God?" and "Why does God allow His people to suffer so greatly?" These are common questions for anyone going through a crisis of faith. The books of 1 and 2 Kings offer true stories that serve to answer these questions. God is real, He keeps His promises, you should keep following God, and sin (specifically the sin of idolatry) leads to captivity and death, but God delivers His people.

Against the backdrop of this larger story is the story of the prophet Elijah in 1 Kings 18 and 19. Elijah received two chapters where he is center stage, and these two chapters are studies in contrast between spiritual highs (chapter 18) and spiritual lows (chapter 19). A person can find themselves in a crisis of faith immediately following a spiritual victory.

The story of Elijah also makes clear the complex nature of a crisis of faith. Spiritual lows are often a mixture of spiritual and physical symptoms and causes, which suggests that surviving a crisis of faith involves caring for both the body and the soul.

Biblical Anthropology

Biblical anthropology describes God's design and intention for human beings. It is a biblical picture of humanity. Some basic facts about human beings should be clearly understood from the first three chapters of Genesis. First, humans were created by God (John 1:3). Second, humans are created without sin and in God's image (Genesis 1:27). Third, humans are created with a body and a soul (Genesis 2:7). Fourth, humans are created male and female (Genesis 1:27). Fifth, humans are created for noble and interconnected purposes: work, worship, and relationship (Genesis 1:28).

Knowing these basic facts about humanity is important. It is like a camping trip for the soul. Sociologists have sought to understand the attraction of camping to modern human beings. Why would someone who has the luxuries of modern life pay money and spend time sleeping outdoors? Of course, those of us who enjoy camping point to the pure enjoyment of being in nature and to the simple pleasures of camping, such as campfires.

Sociologists, on the other hand, tend to explain camping in terms of human development. There was a time when humans were nomadic and primitive. Camping is believed to be a way of reconnecting with primitive humanity: getting back to our roots.

Rehearsing the basic facts of creation is like a camping trip for the soul. Reminding yourself, or being reminded, of where you come from is grounding. It is an exercise in spiritual orientation.

God cares for what He created. You are not just a body. You are a body and a soul. God cares for you as a whole.

Christians are therefore not only concerned with the soul but also with the body. When God created the universe He declared it was good (Genesis 1:31). The body is not inherently bad but rather desires, dispositions, and actions contrary to the character and will of God are sinful.

Where did things go wrong? Genesis 3 describes how sin entered the world. This event is called the fall. Humanity falls into sin, resulting in physical and spiritual separation from the presence of God. This break in relationship results in physical death and suffering.

Sin makes everything difficult. Childbirth is painful. Marriage is hard. Work is frustrating. God warns us, and we (like Adam and Eve) sin anyway. The results have been catastrophic, ongoing, and comprehensive. Everything is negatively affected by sin, but everything is not ruined.

Another paradox of Scripture is that even after the fall, goodness remains. The physical world, despite its hardships and suffering, is filled with beauty. The heavens declare the glory of the Lord despite occasional thunderstorms. Like the Cross, itself a symbol of both life and death, the physical world, on a daily basis, is a reminder of both the goodness of creation and the destruction of sin.

When my daughter was five years old her appendix ruptured. As a result, she spent a week at a children's hospital in Oakland, California. Her mother and I took turns being with her; mom usually took the day shift, and I took the night shift. As you probably know, a hospital is a loud place, a cacophony of human and mechanical sounds. Spending the night in a hospital is a restless ordeal with brief interludes of sleep interrupted by beeps, moans, talking, alarms, and other disruptive sounds.

And so to my surprise, one morning, I awoke to hear something in addition to the usual beeps and voices: the unmistakable sound of a cello being played in the hallway. I walked to the doorway and stood amazed. In the other doorways parents and patients alike investigated the heavenly sound. Some saintly person volunteers their time playing music to bless the sick children and sleepless family members at the children's hospital in Oakland, California.

We live in a fallen world, but there are reminders of our glorious origin. Before there was a curse there was a Garden. We experience cancer and hurricanes but also national parks and symphonies. The Bible explains both the good, the bad, and the ugly of human existence.

An even greater marvel is that humans remain image bearers after the fall. We are ongoing specimens of unique evidence to the glory of the Creator and also to the tragedy of the fall. If nature can be confusing, how much more so humanity. Made in the image of God and yet dead in sin. Humans are a walking contradiction.

Blaise Pascal nailed the paradox of fallen humanity:

> What kind of freak is man! What a novelty he is, how absurd he is, how chaotic and what a mass of contradictions, and yet what a prodigy! He is judge of all things, yet a feeble worm. He is repository of truth, and yet sinks into such doubt and error. He is the glory and the scum of the universe! —*The Mind of Fire*

This contradiction is on full display in the life of Elijah the prophet. One moment he stands alone for God against the four hundred and fifty prophets of Baal, and the next moment he complains to God that he is all alone. One moment Elijah charges toward King Ahab, and the next moment he runs away from Queen Jezebel. Such is humanity, a freak race of fallen image bearers at once both great and wretched.

The Story of Elijah

Elijah was an obscure and unlikely hero from the beginning. First King 17:1 introduces Elijah somewhat abruptly, saying, "Now Elijah the Tishbite"—which just means he was a settler in Gilead. No family history, no basket-in-the-Nile story as with Moses, and no Spirit-filling in the womb as with John the Baptist. Elijah shows up on stage with no opening act, no announcement, and no fanfare, and this matter-of-fact introduction colors the remainder of his ministry.

At times Elijah is a model of obedience. God says, "Arise, go to Zarephath" and Elijah "arose and went to Zarephath" (vv. 9–10). Elijah's moments of obedience do not spare him a crisis of faith.

Elijah is most famous for his showdown with the prophets of Baal on Mount Carmel as recorded in 1 Kings 18:20–40. The evil king of Israel (Ahab) and his idolatrous wife (Jezebel) promoted idol worship in Israel. The totality of Ahab's apostasy is made evident in the short summary of his religious actions upon his ascension to the kingship and marriage to Jezebel: "He erected an altar for Baal in the house of Baal, which he built in Samaria" (1 Kings 16:32). The king of God's people married a pagan wife and ran a house church to a false god that was zealously evangelistic for a foreign religion. This is total depravity.

Jezebel was a Phoenician princess. She executed the prophets of Yahweh (1 Kings 18:13). Ahab did not like Elijah and bullied him as the "troubler of Israel" (v. 17). Jezebel hated Elijah and wanted him dead.

On Mount Carmel, Elijah and Ahab fight a kind of proxy war; the real showdown is between Yahweh and Baal. Yahweh has one hero prophet (foreshadowing), and Baal has four hundred and fifty prophets. The rules are simple: One altar for Baal and one for Yahweh. Each altar has a bull sacrifice. Whichever God sends fire from heaven to consume the sacrifice wins and deserves to be worshipped.

The prophets of Baal go first. They call out from morning until noon, but no one answers. As evidence that trash talking can be biblical, Elijah begins to mock the prophets of Baal, saying:

Cry aloud, for he is a god. Either he is musing, or he is relieving himself, or he is on a journey, or perhaps he is asleep and must be awakened. —v. 27

Refusing to give up, the prophets of Baal dance and cut themselves. Their scene is one of commotion and blood, but no fire. This image of humans bleeding and calling out to false gods who do not answer is the perfect picture of idol worship. False religion always demands that humans become their own sacrifice. On Mount Carmel and everywhere else that it is practiced, false religion ends in chaos, frustration, and death. In summary, all their efforts produced "no voice. No one answered; no one paid attention" (v. 29).

After the prophets of Baal, it was Elijah's turn to call down fire:

O Lord, God of Abraham, Isaac, and Israel, let it be known this day that you are God in Israel, and that I am your servant, and that I have done all these things at your word. Answer me, O Lord, answer me, that this people may know that you, O Lord, are God, and that you have turned their hearts back. —vv. 36–37

Worship of Yahweh looked different from the worship of Baal. There was no commotion or theatrics. There was a simple reminder of God's covenant faithfulness and His Word along with an expressed desire for hearts to be turned to God.

After Elijah said these words "the fire of the Lord fell" (v. 38). Elijah commanded the people to seize the prophets of Baal. He slaughtered them at the brook of Kishon. God's judgment through God's prophet turned the hearts of God's people to God. After a long drought it started to rain!

It would have been a Hollywood ending, but it was not over. The story takes a sudden and unexpected turn. Jezebel heard what happened on Mount Carmel and in retaliation sends assassins to kill Elijah. In fear for his life, Elijah goes on the run.

The man who called down fire from heaven finds a tree, sits down, and prays a different kind of prayer, "It is enough; now, O Lord, take away my life, for I am no better than my fathers" (1 Kings 19:4).

It doesn't make sense. Why would Elijah run from the assassins into the wilderness fearing death only to ask God to take his life? Does he want to live or does he want to die? We can learn from Elijah's confusion. You probably will not do your best thinking during a crisis of faith. Crisis clouds thinking and distorts perspective.

Christians should plan ahead of time how to respond to a crisis of faith. There is an old proverb, which says the best time to plant a tree is twenty years ago, and the next best time to plant a tree is today! During a crisis of faith, you often cannot trust your own judgment. Most of us do not plan ahead for a crisis of faith. Thankfully it is never too late to respond faithfully and make wise decisions.

Giving Up

On the run, Elijah is a case study in the symptoms of spiritual defeat. Afraid and troubled, the once great prophet heads into the desert and sits under a broom tree (v. 5). Elijah essentially quit the prophet business. He is not only running away from Jezebel, he is running from God.

There is always a spiritual dimension to human suffering. Trouble is never only about what can be seen with eyes and touched with hands. Sometimes the battle *involves* flesh and blood, but the battle is not *only* or *ultimately* about flesh and blood.

Elijah hid under a broom tree, good for shade in the desert and a fitting metaphor for attempts to run from God. Adam and Eve tried to hide from God. Elijah did the same thing. We are no different. We find broom trees and hide, but our broom trees may take the form of old relationships, destructive habits, self-medication, or entertainment. In a crisis of faith, you are more likely to run away from God to people and things that cannot save and will not satisfy.

Elijah did not just quit. He wanted to die. To his credit, and for our instruction, Elijah understood that his life was not his to take. As more proof that faith and doubt coexist, Elijah asked God to take his life. He doubted God, but at the same time he believed God was in control of life and death.

It is common in a crisis of faith to think death would be preferable to life. In his trials, Job asked, "Why did I not die at birth, come out from the womb and expire?" (Job 3:11). Rebekah said, "I loathe my life" (Genesis 27:46), and Jonah prayed, "O Lord, please take my life from me, for it is better for me to die than to live" (Jonah 4:3). Paul and his companions despaired of life itself (2 Corinthians 1:8).

In their despair, each of these people cried out to God. You are never alone. He is always there to hear you and comfort you.

If you have thought about killing yourself or made plans to do so, please get help. Talk to someone. Remember that your life is not yours to take. You belong to God. You are still made in God's image. No matter how bad things may seem, you still have worth, meaning, and value.

Elijah, Rebekah, Jonah, and Paul and his companions knew what modern culture avoids: suicide is murder. Killing a person unjustly is murder, whether that person is you or someone else. In times past, Christians wrongly thought suicide was the unpardonable sin. Today the pendulum has swung to the opposite extreme, and suicide is rarely called a sin at all.

The truth is in the middle. Suicide is not the unpardonable sin, but it is a sin. Mental health issues often play a part in suicide, but they do not absolve a person before God of sin.

In addition to being afraid, troubled, and wanting to die, Elijah also feels alone. Twice in the story he says, "I, even I only," as he talks to

God (1 Kings 19:10 and 14). Elijah felt alone, and this too is common during a crisis of faith.

Oftentimes loneliness is a self-fulfilling prophecy. Elijah was traveling with a servant, but left him to run (alone) into the desert. Was he alone? Yes, but it was his own fault! God reminded Elijah that there were seven thousand other people in his corner (v. 18). In fact, Paul uses this story in Romans to remind Christians that God keeps His promises and is building His church (Romans 11:1–6).

In a crisis of faith, avoid distancing yourself from the very people God has provided to stand with you in times of uncertainty. You are not alone. God is with you, and God has people (the church) intended to support you in your hardships.

One lie in particular that unnecessarily prolongs a crisis of faith is a lie that Elijah essentially told himself: No one knows how I feel. Elijah was deep in self-deception and self-pity until God pointed out the reality of the situation. There were others. In fact, God has prepared people around you to minister to you in your crisis because they have experienced a similar crisis (2 Corinthians 1:3–11).

Not only did Elijah feel alone, he felt betrayed by God. Twice Elijah reminded God of his faithful service and jealousy for God. The implication is obvious: *God, I did my job, and You didn't do yours.* When life circumstances fail to meet expectations, a common response is to feel as though God has let us down.

Part of this is due to bad theology in the church. The so-called prosperity gospel promises that in return for your faith God will give health, wealth, and prosperity. There are three fundamental problems with this theology that prolong a crisis of faith. First, Jesus is the most faithful person to have ever lived—sinless, in fact—and yet he was a man of sorrow, associated with grief, and despised and rejected. Sometimes our trials are the results of our sinful decisions, but other times, they are just the result of living in a fallen world.

Second, the prosperity gospel also commits the same sin as the prodigal son, who impatiently demanded an early inheritance. The prodigal son is a model of unbelief. He did not trust his father to give him good things at the right time. After learning the cost of impatience, the son returned to the father, whose running welcome and open arms illustrate the glory of saving grace.

God does promises a time when our glorified bodies will no longer suffer, streets are paved with gold, and tears cease. These promises are like keys, and the keys belong to a kingdom that is not of this world. We will get our inheritance when we are united with the Son in the Father's good timing.

Lastly, the prosperity gospel replaces the gospel of grace with a gospel of karma. All religion is based on either karma or grace. Karma is getting what you deserve, and grace is getting good things you do not deserve. Salvation is by grace alone; it is undeserved favor with God earned by Jesus, and not by you. The prosperity gospel is really more like Prosperity Karma; do enough good (believe, give, etc.), and God is somehow obligated to give you good things in return. That is karma, not grace.

In a crisis of faith, ask yourself whether or not you have replaced biblical grace with worldly karma. If you believe you deserve something as the result of your faith you will be endlessly disappointed. On the other hand, if you believe you deserve hell, and instead through Christ you have been given eternal life, your crisis of faith will be abated by a profound sense of thanksgiving.

Elijah complains to God, appearing to believe that his faithfulness was going unrewarded. How misguided and yet how common. We think if we raise our kids in a Christian home and teach them about Jesus, take them to church, and seek to disciple them in the faith, that somehow God owes us their salvation or safety. By God's grace this is often the case, but there are no guarantees. We think if we work hard and handle our money wisely we will be spared financial hardships, but God never made those promises.

So often our crisis of faith is based on the misguided assumption that God owes us something. In reality, God promises that in this life we will suffer. That is a promise we do not like to claim.

Elijah felt like giving up. His crisis of faith involved a sense of fear, trouble, hopelessness, loneliness, and disappointment. And yet we know that Elijah made it through his crisis of faith. In this next section we will look at how God enabled Elijah to make it through the storm and come out safely on the other side.

Going On When You Feel Like Giving Up

Elijah did not stay under the broom tree. What lessons can we learn
from Elijah that will enable us to go on when we feel like giving up?

1. **First, God hears.** Perhaps the first lesson from Elijah is the
    necessity of prayer when we least feel like praying. Elijah talked
    to God. Although he prayed what is likely the most pitiful
    prayer in the whole Bible, he did pray! Elijah asked God to take
    his life. What can we possibly learn from this sorry attempt at
    communicating with God?

    God hears broken prayers. He sees us on our knees, bro-
    kenhearted, without words to express our sorrow. He hears par-
    ents sobbing and broken cries over wayward children. He sees
    us hurting and betrayed. He knows how that feels. He listens
    to broken people whose realities fall far short of their dreams.

2. **Second, God listens.** Everything else God does in Elijah's life
    during his crisis of faith is the result of Elijah talking to God
    about his sorrow. Everything good starts with prayer. God leads
    us to pray, and then through our prayer, He does His good
    work. We want faith-filled prayers, but when you lack faith,
    pray anyway. James says that if we draw near to God, He will
    draw near to us (James 4:8). In drawing near to God, and in
    His drawing near to us, we often find our faith building, grow-
    ing, and strengthening.

    Don't wait until the crisis of faith is over to start praying.
    Imagine the folly of a person waiting to see a doctor until they
    are done being sick. It would make no sense, and neither does
    avoiding God as though He doesn't already know the angles
    and texture of your despondency. Elijah teaches us not to wait,
    to go to God, and to pray honest prayers.

3. **Third, God cares for the whole person.** Just as God created
    human beings with a body and a soul, so He ministers to
    human beings both physically and spiritually. Read the follow-
    ing description of God's ministry to Elijah:

    And he lay down and slept under a broom tree. And behold,
    an angel touched him and said to him, "Arise and eat." And he

looked, and behold, there was at his head a cake baked on hot stones and a jar of water. And he ate and drank and lay down again. And the angel of the Lord came again a second time and touched him and said, "Arise and eat, for the journey is too great for you." And he arose and ate and drank, and went in the strength of that food forty days and forty nights to Horeb, the mount of God. —1 Kings 19:5–8

God himself ministers to Elijah's physical needs with water, food, and rest.[4] A crisis of faith can be caused, or exacerbated, by neglecting basic physical needs. Dehydration, hunger, and exhaustion will make it hard to take thoughts captive and wage war against the flesh. Sometimes the most spiritual thing you can do is eat a good meal, drink water, and take a nap.

God's character, example, and commands are instructive for the church in how to care well for its members during a crisis of faith. Sharing a book, sermon, podcast, or Bible verse can be a lifeline for the soul. Such resources are fuel for faith and help us to live to fight another day. Man does not live by bread alone.

And yet the story of Elijah reminds us that the circumstances of crisis must inform and direct our care. The tired new parents, for instance, probably need meals delivered before anything else. The discouraged parent may need free babysitting and a night out more than a lecture on parenting. The grieving widow may need an invitation to dinner more than merely a passing word of encouragement.

In leadership theory there is something called the grand gesture, which is a special visible act that intentionally communicates or reinforces a principle, vision, or mission. When Jesus washed the disciple's feet, it was a jaw-dropping, show-stopping gesture that communicated both the nature of servant leadership and Jesus' ultimate mission to wash His disciples clean from sin.

Ron Chernow's best-selling biography *Alexander Hamilton* tells the story of George Washington addressing Continental

---

[4] For evidence that the Angel of the Lord is the Lord himself, see Judges 13.

Army officers on March 15, 1783. At this point the war was all but won, but the soldiers were frustrated because they had not been paid. These soldiers made a great sacrifice, but it was a sacrifice Washington himself had also made: Washington never received a salary for commanding the revolutionary forces, and his duties had taken a physical toll. As Washington spoke to the angry officers, he paused for a moment in order to put on his reading glasses, which he did not normally wear. Chernow calls this moment "the most famous coup de théâtre," as Washington said, "You will permit me to put on my spectacles, for I have not only grown gray but almost blind in service to my country." Washington's grand gesture powerfully reminded the soldiers that their leader shared in their suffering. The soldiers grew quiet with shame. Washington had made his point.

Service is the grand gesture. Christian service requires wisdom to do the right things at the right time in the right ways. If you are serving someone in a crisis of faith, prioritize their need over your preference. You may prefer to share a sermon, but if they need a meal, it will not help them cope with the physical aspects of a crisis of faith. If you are going through a crisis of faith, communicate your needs to your local church and have the humility to receive God's ministry to you through his people.

4. **Fourth, God pursues.** God gets Elijah through his crisis of faith through prayer, ministering to Elijah's needs, and also by pursuing Elijah. Elijah is running away from God, but God is running toward Elijah. Twice God asks Elijah, "What are you doing here?" (1 Kings 19:9 and 13).

Doubt often feels as though God is abandoning us, or even that we deserve to be abandoned—as though the perfect obedience and righteousness of Christ had not been applied to our account! God is not abandoning us. In fact, He is pursuing us!

"The Hound of Heaven," a nineteenth-century poem by Francis Thompson, describes a man on the run from God:

I fled Him, down the nights and down the days;
I fled Him, down the arches of the years;

I fled Him, down the labyrinthine ways
Of my own mind; and in the mist of tears
I hid from Him, and under running laughter.

In the poem, God is constantly present. He reminds the wayward man that ultimate rest and peace are only found in Him. God is the greatest good man can seek:

Ah fondest, blindest, weakest,
I am He Whom thou seekest!

The story of Elijah on the run from Jezebel is a reminder that in a crisis of faith God is present and in pursuit. This same point is made by another poet:

Where shall I go from your Spirit? Or where shall I flee from your presence? If I ascend to heaven, you are there! If I make my bed in Sheol, you are there! If I take the wings of the morning and dwell in the uttermost parts of the sea, even there your hand shall lead me, and your right hand shall hold me. If I say, "Surely the darkness shall cover me, and the light about me be night," even the darkness is not dark to you; the night is bright as the day, for darkness is as light with you. —Psalm 139:7–12

There are many ways you probably sense the pursuit of God—sorrow over sin, the desire to return to obedience (or at least the desire *to desire* such a return!), verses you learned as a child that pop into your head as you try to live your own way. The Good Shepherd goes after the sheep.

What does this mean for you in a crisis of faith? As they say on *Star Trek: The Next Generation*, "Resistance is futile." If you have come to saving faith, you belong to God. He purchased you. He will not lose you.

This is comforting. However, the counterbalancing exhortation is that we should flee to God and not run away from

God. In fact, the fear of the Lord kicks in during a crisis of faith as a response to God's loving pursuit. His kindness leads us to repentance (Romans 2:4).

Elijah is able to go on when he feels like giving up because God hears his broken prayer, ministers to his needs, and pursues him. But the story of Elijah's return centers squarely on the importance of God's Word.

Remember that on Mount Carmel the prophets of Baal cried out to Baal, "But there was no voice. No one answered; no one paid attention" (1 Kings 18:29). In contrast to Baal, God hears Elijah whether he is on Mount Carmel, under the broom tree, or hiding in a cave. God hears His children whether they pray in great faith or in great doubt.

5. **Fifth, God revives.** God ministers to Elijah and in so doing He begins the process of reviving Elijah. God does more than minister to Elijah's needs, but He does not do less. In our fight against unbelief, the church is armed with both words of truth and acts of charity.

A crisis of faith involves the whole person, body and soul. This means there are times to consult doctors, nutritionists, counselors, and other health care providers. Years ago, a young student at a Christian college came into my office unannounced after a recent mission trip. He paced in front of my desk, telling me God was speaking to him and telling him details about the second coming of Jesus. Of course, none of this was true. I immediately suspected this young man was in the throes of a psychotic episode. I asked him, "Do you know who would love to hear this story? The campus physician!" He smiled and agreed to walk with me to the campus physician, who promptly addressed the underlying physical aspects of this student's mental breakdown. The young man hadn't slept or eaten in days.

Don't assume that a crisis of faith is all about Scripture, doctrine, or spiritual warfare. It may have much to do with hunger, sleeplessness, exhaustion, dehydration, or other physical aspects of the fall. Yes, sin is the *ultimate* cause. But the *immediate* cause may require simple acts of physical care. God uses a variety of means to revive His people both physically and spiritually according to His Word.

6. **Sixth, God speaks.** God not only hears, ministers, and pursues, but He also speaks. More than anything else, God's Word will get you through a crisis of faith. God speaks six times in the story of Elijah on the run from God in 1 Kings 19.

The most famous of these moments comes when God meets with Elijah on Mount Horeb, the "Mount of God," elsewhere called Mount Sinai:

And behold, the Lord passed by, and a great and strong wind tore the mountains and broke in pieces the rocks before the Lord, but the Lord was not in the wind. And after the wind an earthquake, but the Lord was not in the earthquake. And after the earthquake a fire, but the Lord was not in the fire. And after the fire the sound of a low whisper. —vv. 11–12

The text says God passed by Elijah in the same way he passed by Moses in Exodus 34. This detail reminds God's people that God had not changed. Even when in captivity, as Israel was when they received these books, God had not changed, His covenant promises had not changed, and His character had not changed.

Oftentimes we read such Old Testament passages and wish we could have mountaintop experiences with God such as Moses and Elijah had. However, we have something better. The author of Hebrews connects Jesus with these Old Testament scenes by declaring Jesus to be the God who is the same yesterday, today, and forever (Hebrews 13:8). It is not a stretch to say that Jesus met with both Moses and Elijah, but they wouldn't have known His name or seen His face; they experienced only a passing brush with the preincarnate Savior.

We get to know His name! In the Gospels we see Him more clearly than either Moses or Elijah. The angel of the Lord who ministered to Elijah, the Good Shepherd who pursued Elijah, has become known to us in Jesus Christ and has been revealed for us to behold and worship. We do not go to a mountain, but to a Person—the second Person of the Trinity, God the Son. By the power of the Holy Spirit we are drawn to Him and receive His words according to the eternal plan of the Father.

We are a part of this story. God continues to guide us through His Word. It says God was not in the wind, the earthquake, or the fire. After these things there was a soft whisper, or literally, a still, small voice.

Does this mean that if we are quiet we will hear God's voice? That does not seem to be the point of the passage. In fact, Elijah immediately wraps his face in his cloak and ignores God!

Life is full of distractions. In a crisis of faith, rocks break, the earth moves, and fires rage. Life is unsettled. In the confusion and chaos of life, going to the Word of God is how we hear God's voice.

The way to go on when you feel like giving up is by paying attention to the unchanging God and His unchanging Word. The psalmist says, "Forever, O Lord, your word is firmly fixed in the heavens" (Psalm 119:89). Jesus says God's word cannot be broken (John 10:35). Jesus says that heaven and earth will pass away but His words will not pass away (Matthew 24:35).

On January 7, 1855, Charles Spurgeon preached a sermon on the words from the prophet Malachi, "For I the Lord do not change" (Malachi 3:6). Speaking of the human desire for something permanent, stable, and transcendent in an ever-changing world, Spurgeon declared, "I want immutable things: and I find that I have immutable promises when I turn to the Bible."

In a crisis of faith, the feeling of spiritual disorientation ceases as we gather our bearings according to the Bible, God's unchanging Word. Your quiet times are never more important than when you doubt. You will make it through a crisis of faith if you focus on what God has said. He speaks in His Word.

7. **Seventh, God has everything under control**. What initially drove Elijah into the desert was, by his own admission, a sinful

sense of fear and abandonment. But God comforts Elijah by reminding Him that he is sovereign and has everything under control:

> And the Lord said to him, "Go, return on your way to the wilderness of Damascus. And when you arrive, you shall anoint Hazael to be king over Syria. And Jehu the son of Nimshi you shall anoint to be king over Israel, and Elisha the son of Shaphat of Abel-meholah you shall anoint to be prophet in your place. And the one who escapes from the sword of Hazael shall Jehu put to death, and the one who escapes from the sword of Jehu shall Elisha put to death. Yet I will leave seven thousand in Israel, all the knees that have not bowed to Baal, and every mouth that has not kissed him." —1 Kings 19:15–18

Elijah felt alone, but he was never alone. During his crisis of faith there were seven thousand other people who were faithful to Yahweh. God speaks the truth in love.

In a crisis of faith, people are often both a blessing and a curse. In whatever crisis you may go through, people are inevitably a causal part of the crisis.

At the same time, God's people are a vital part of your road to recovery. Do not make the mistake of distancing yourself from healthy Christ-centered relationships for the sake of the "Ahabs" and "Jezebels" of the world. Yes, there is real evil. But there is also profound goodness in the body of Christ. These relationships will help you survive a crisis of faith.

All along, God had it under control. The doctrine of God's sovereignty is perhaps the most precious doctrine to which a believer clings during a crisis of faith. Things may appear to be chaotic and random, but events are unfolding according to God's plan. He knows the end from the beginning and has the final say on whatever takes place.

Take for example a crisis of faith related to a fear of death. Elijah, after all, was running for his life. He feared Jezebel and ran for his life, only to ask God to kill him! A crisis of faith weakens both our spiritual resolve and often our reasoning as well.

In the Book of Acts there is a powerful statement about David in regard to the fear of death. It says, "For David, after he had served the purpose of God in his own generation, fell asleep and was laid with his fathers and saw corruption, but he whom God raised up did not see corruption" (Acts 13:36–37). These verses make a profound point about death, a common source of anxiety and fear.

David did not die until he had fulfilled all of God's purposes for his life. You will not die until you fulfill God's purposes for your life. The beginning and ending of life is demarcated by the eternal purposes of God. God's sovereign care applies to all people, not just kings. His purposes for us are often mysterious and may not coincide with our preferences. Nevertheless, a crisis of faith related to a fear of death begins to unravel in the light of this powerful truth: God is in control.

A Long and Complicated Recovery

Coming back from a crisis of faith is usually not instantaneous. The duration between Elijah's Mount Carmel experience and the end of his crisis of faith was over a month-and-a-half long, at least. It may take some time to make it through your crisis of faith.

Every family that has ever taken a road trip with kids knows the question, "Are we there yet?" The question itself is a classic trope of impatience during a journey. Thanks to GPS and other mapping systems, adults (and children) can now look and see exactly how much longer it will take to reach the intended destination.

The journey back from a crisis of faith is one where you may find yourself asking, "How long?" and, "Are we there yet?" In 1 Kings 19, God gives Elijah six clear tasks to do that would led him out of the literal (and figurative) wilderness of his wandering. In other words, freedom is a process.

Salvation is instantaneous in terms of our standing before God, but sanctification is an ongoing and often grueling process. God regards us as holy in Christ, but the process of being transformed in Christ-likeness takes time, energy, and sacrifice. Dying to self is not instantaneous. Sanctification is a journey we take one step at a time.

This doesn't mean there are not things you can do immediately to begin the journey back from a crisis of faith. Repentance is one step you can take right away. Decide to turn from any sin that is associated with your crisis of faith. For Elijah, it was running from God's people and ignoring God's Word. His immediate step of obedience was listening to God and going home.

C. S. Lewis says in *Mere Christianity*, "Repentance is no fun at all. ... It means killing part of yourself, undergoing a kind of death." Many churches have stopped talking about repentance for this very reason. However, apart from repentance, there is no going to God. Lewis continues, "If you ask God to take you back without it, you are really asking Him to let you go back without going back."

The decision to do something may be instantaneous, but the process takes time. A crisis of faith associated with an intellectual question or objection may take time to research, but the *decision* to do the research and seek answers is immediate. A crisis of faith related to a personal trauma may take counseling, but the decision to get counseling is immediate. The immediate step is the decision to go in the right direction.

The journey takes time and requires a healthy understanding of divine sovereignty and human responsibility. God's sovereignty does not negate human responsibility. Instead, our action is made possible by God's Spirit through the power of His Word. God tells Elijah what to do, and His Spirit empowers Elijah to obey, but Elijah must exercise his faith, control himself, and obey. Elijah reminds us that sanctification is about the direction of our life, not the perfection of our life.

Making it back from a crisis of faith is an illustration of what James 2 describes as faith working itself out in obedience. Charles Spurgeon puts it this way: "The best and the wisest thing in the world is to work as if it all depended upon you, and then trust in God, knowing that it all depends upon Him." Commit yourself to prayer and other spiritual disciplines, work hard, and trust God.

Jesus Is the Hero

The story of Elijah reminds us that Jesus is the only hero. A crisis of faith is sometimes initiated when spiritual leaders let us down. Elijah is a spiritual leader, who in one moment is mighty in the Lord and in the next is running, hiding, doubting, and pointing fingers. People will let you down. Even the best Christian leader is a fallen leader.

Jesus is the only sinless exception. He is the only hero. In Judges 13 we see that Jesus is the Angel of the Lord. At the transfiguration, Jesus is identified as the glory cloud of God (Matthew 17: 2–5). Jesus is the Good Shepherd who pursues His sheep (John 10:11–18). Jesus is the Word of the Lord incarnate (John 1:14) who brings us eternal life (John 10:10). The New Testament makes it clear: Jesus passed by Elijah on the mountain and met with Elijah in the cave.

Going on when you feel like giving up starts with going in faith to Jesus. Looking to Jesus is how you make it through a crisis of faith. More than that, it is the substance and essence of the Christian life.

You are not the hero of the story. A crisis of faith can serve many useful purposes, such as purging notions of self-grandeur and curing messiah complexes. Before a crisis of faith, you may idolize people and think highly of yourself. After a crisis of faith, you are less likely to put people on a pedestal and increasingly likely to humble yourself in your own self-assessment.

Like in the lyrics of the classic children's song "Jesus Loves Me," a crisis of faith reminds us we "are weak, but He is strong." We are physically and spiritually weak. A crisis of faith exposes our daily need for a Savior to walk with us, strengthen us, and save us.

Jesus is the only hero.

Chapter 6

David: How Long, O Lord?

So far we have seen that saving faith is like a dimmer switch. Doubt and faith coexist in the life of a believer. Times of doubt are common, but God has ways to strengthen our faith and see us through.

What about trials where there is no end in sight? When hardships are ongoing and suffering is lifelong? How do you maintain hope and cling to faith when circumstances are especially bleak and there is no light at the end of the tunnel? Eighteenth-century minister and theologian Andrew Fuller preached that it's during the longest trials when we are in the greatest danger of fainting.

If this is your situation, there is hope. You are certainly not alone. Others have lived faithful, productive, and joyful Christian lives while at the same time enduring lifelong affliction, persecution, hardship, and downright misery. There is joy to be had in the darkest valleys. Christ is often most sweet when life is most bitter.

Psalm 23 is one of the most famous passages of Scripture. It describes life as "the valley of the shadow of death" (v. 4). Jesus is the Good Shepherd who walks in the valley, revives us along the way, and prepares a reward for us after our journey in the valley is over. A walk is a fitting metaphor used often in Scripture for life. We prefer to drive or fly long distances. Putting one foot in front of the other over long distances takes time and tenacity.

Time Warp

We have all had an experience when time seemed to stand still. During moments of stress, discomfort, and hardship, time moves slowly. Conversely, time flies when you're having fun! Charles Spurgeon says more poetically in his book *Treasury of David*, "Time flies with full-fledged wing in our summer days, but in our winters he flutters painfully." This peculiar experience of time slowing down and seeming to stand still is what I mean by *time warp*.

The phenomenon of time warp has been attributed to everything from adrenaline to increased activity in the amygdala, the area of the brain responsible for emotions and memory. Perhaps God designed us to lay down extra memories during times of high emotional stress in order to learn lessons that would increase survival and well-being. Few of us would want to relive a traumatic experience.

The residual experience of emotions associated with traumatic memories as the result of increased activity in the amygdala may explain other phenomenon, such as intuition and déjà vu. When a person says, "I have a bad feeling about this," or, "This seems familiar," it may be an association between current sensations and past sensations (memory).

The neurological and psychological aspects of time warp are interesting, but the spiritual dimensions are varied and complex. The hardest year of your life will probably seem like the longest. The Bible is not silent on this issue; Psalm 13 gives pointed instruction for managing emotions in the midst of time warp that will help you make it through a crisis of faith.

Asking the Same Questions

God empowers us to affect many aspects of life, but there are some aspects entirely outside of our control. Assuming you are taking wise steps to address those issues within your control, a crisis of faith where time seems to be standing still can be positively affected by adopting David's perspective in Psalm 13:

> How long, O Lord? Will you forget me forever? How long will you hide your face from me? How long must I take counsel in my soul and have sorrow in my heart all the day? How long shall my enemy be exalted over me? Consider and answer me,

O Lord my God; light up my eyes, lest I sleep the sleep of death, lest my enemy say, "I have prevailed over him," lest my foes rejoice because I am shaken. But I have trusted in your steadfast love; my heart shall rejoice in your salvation. I will sing to the Lord, because he has dealt bountifully with me.

We do not know the circumstances that led David to write this psalm. He begins the psalm anxious, exhausted, and desperate. He ends the psalm hopeful, joyful, and thankful. It is a case study in surviving a crisis of faith and making it back safely into the restful arms of the Shepherd.

Four times David asks variations of the same question: *How long?* The worst part of a crisis of faith is not knowing when it will end. David asks God, "Will you forget me forever?" Sometimes it seems like a crisis of faith will never end.

It is good that we do not know the specific context of Psalm 13 because it applies to whatever crisis you're going through. Job 5:7 says, "Man is born to trouble as the sparks fly upward," and Job 14:1 says that life is "few of days and full of trouble." Given that life is short and difficult, God's people need songs like Psalm 13 that give words to our doubts, anxiety, and desperation. These psalms were prayers sung by God's people in times of trouble.

Charles Spurgeon calls Psalm 13 the Howling Psalm and instructs the reader to see in David "a deep searching of heart." The psalm begins with a deep sense of abandonment and ends with confidence in God. There is this trajectory from despair to hope that every Christian in crisis longs to experience. Martin Luther says Psalm 13 shows that hope despairs, and despair hopes.

David feels as though God has forgotten him or is hiding from him. This cry of anguish ("How long?") resonates because of its candor and transparency. How rare for human leaders to be this vulnerable and humble. David displays a profound insight into the secret life of a believer during a crisis of faith. Despite his formidable hardships, David wants to trust in God.

We see in David a tension between feeling as though you can't go on and feeling as though you must go on. David is aware of his own weakness. Have you ever tried to hold on to something but could feel yourself losing your grip? In a crisis of faith, we feel at once both the desire to go on and the desire to give up: "Wretched man that I am! Who will deliver me from this body of death?" (Romans 7:24)

David had enemies—rivals, foreign threats, family conflict, and internal divisions. He was a man after God's own heart (1 Samuel 13:14), but he was also a murderer (2 Samuel 11—12), adulterer (2 Samuel 11), and polygamist (2 Samuel 5:13). His life was full of hardships, many of which were undoubtedly the result of his own sinful decisions. A crisis of faith is usually complicated and almost always messy.

Nevertheless, David is a believer who maintains an ardent desire to be faithful to God. What we see in Psalm 13 is the importance of intentional faith. Passivity is waiting for things to change before you believe. Intentionality is believing while you work and pray for things to change.

Intentionality does not come naturally. Remember the old arcade game Whac-A-Mole? The goal was to hit mechanical moles with a cushioned mallet. It has become a metaphor for futility. The reactionary life feels like Whac-A-Mole. The result is spiritual exhaustion as day after day you hit the same targets mechanically, thoughtlessly, and joylessly over and over again. It is a kind of existential slavery. The Book of Ecclesiastes says that the natural man lives a life of vanity and futility apart from God.

Living a reactionary life is simply going through the motions. When a Christian allows himself or herself to drift from intentionality, it can induce a crisis of faith. Monotony drains the meaning and sucks the joy out of life. People, places, and activities that once held value seem empty. The dungeon of despair can be a place of one's own making.

On the other hand, a life of intentionality is liberating. Whether or not life circumstances change, there is dignity and value in achieving daily goals. Humans are made in the image of God to worship, work, create, and relate. The intentional life is the outworking of these innate desires that make us human.

The human spirit is virtue in action. To live an intentional life is to be human. To drift into a reactionary existence is to live by instinct and Pavlovian response *like an animal*.

Sin is dehumanizing. It hides the evidence of our humanity. In the story of David and Goliath, Goliath is described as coming out in scales of armor (1 Samuel 17:5). Goliath is pictured as a snake-like instrument of Satan.[1] His humanity covered by sinfulness, Goliath asks, "Am I a dog?" (v. 43). He seems to know the tragedy of his sinful devolution.

If you are a Christian living a reactionary life and are experiencing a crisis of faith, there is freedom to be found through simple and practical steps toward intentionality. If your crisis of faith is related to finances, make an appointment to see a financial advisor or take a money management course. If your crisis of faith is related to parenting, talk to your church leaders about recommending a good book on parenting. Better yet, sit down with an older couple at church that has wisdom and maturity, and learn from them. If your crisis of faith is emotional, make an appointment to see a Christian counselor.

Doing what you need to do is both spiritually mature and emotionally energizing during a crisis of faith. At some point you go from feeling helpless to hopeful. On any given day there is work to be done and joy to be had in doing the work.

Work is a tremendous blessing. This may be your occupation (i.e., what you get paid to do) or simply the tasks you accomplish as part of your daily life (i.e., cleaning the house or mowing the yard). Life is meaningful in part because of work.

Work is meaningful when it is done with excellence, in community, for God's glory, and in a spirit of gratitude. Such work is worshipful. Paul says, "Whatever you do, do all to the glory of God" (1 Corinthians 10:31). Work that is done simply for money or self-promotion is isolating. If work is shoddy or half-hearted then it will fail to be meaningful. Day after day of meaningless work is sure to produce a crisis of faith. If you only work to pay bills or someday retire, then work becomes drudgery. Drudgery induces a sense of meaninglessness and despair: a crisis of faith.

In the Garden of Eden, God gave Adam and Eve work. Before sin entered the world, humans worked. In the relationship of marriage, Adam and Eve were to spread God's image through childbearing.

---

[1] Peter Leithart, *A House for My Name: A Survey of the Old Testament* (Moscow, ID: Canon Press, 2004), 141.

Together they cultivated and kept the garden (Genesis 2:7–9, 15). Adam and Eve, equally created in God's image with unique roles and responsibilities, had the noble work of multiplying, filling the earth, subduing it, and ruling over every living thing that moves on the earth (Genesis 1:27–28). Work is not the result of sin.

After sin enters the world, work becomes hard, frustrating, and relationally difficult (Genesis 3:16–18). Work in a fallen world is often plagued by anxiety related to limited time and resources (v. 19). The work of human relationships (e.g., parenting, marriage, friendships) is also negatively affected by the fall (v. 16).

Work is not the problem; sin is the problem. If work is the problem, then winning the lottery and retiring is the solution. It is common for working adults to have the goal of one day not working, as though the goal of life is getting out of work! No wonder that for many Christians work becomes a place of hopelessness and soul-crushing despair resulting in a crisis of faith.

Do you see work as a noble expression of God's image? Do you see your work as worship? Do you approach your work in gratitude? Do you work "as for the Lord" (Colossians 3:23)? The goal of life should not be to get out of work. In fact, eternity itself will be a place of worshipful work.

How do you imagine eternity? Floating around like a ghost on a cloud? Perhaps you imagine an endless Christian worship concert. The biblical picture is gloriously better and far more interesting than these modern pictures.

Eternal life—what we commonly call heaven—is actually a new earth with a new heaven. The redeemed possess new bodies fit for eternity (Revelation 21). The Bible describes the new earth in many of the same ways it described Eden in Genesis. There is a river (Genesis 2:10 and Revelation 22:1), a Tree of Life (Genesis 2:16–17 and Revelation 22:2), a groom (Adam and Christ), and his bride (Eve and the church).

God is the focus of heaven: Jesus is the light, life, and living water. The imagery is present, and so is the One to whom it all points. If Eden is the best indication of what we will be doing on the new earth, heaven will be a place of worshipful work as we cultivate a new earth in sinless community for God's glory with immense gratitude.

In a crisis of faith, doubt tempts us to feel that daily tasks are meaningless. God calls us to imagine what was and what will be as a motivation to live meaningfully between the times. Small gestures of intentionality reflect the *imago Dei* (image of God). God is in control. We are made in God's image. Exerting some level of control (as ordained by God) is one way in which we strive to be like our heavenly Father. It provides some light in times of darkness and transforms daily tasks into times of worshipful communion *coram Deo* (in the presence of God).

More than a job, God gives us each a calling. If all life is worship, as Paul says in Colossians 3:23 and 1 Corinthians 10:31, then there is no division between sacred and secular. The call and vocation of a pastor is no more spiritual than the calling and vocation of a plumber, stay-at-home parent, or salesperson. Workers—wherever they work—who use their skills in community as image bearers, valuing other image bearers with good work and fairness (i.e., loving your neighbor as yourself), working as unto the Lord with gratitude, are as much in the ministry of the kingdom as any pastor or missionary.

A crisis of faith leaves a person feeling out of control, daily tasks lose meaning, and the drudgery of work exacerbates the season of doubt. Taking joy in work and exerting control over that which is under your control will give you a sense of value and purpose as God intended. Do not confuse sovereignty with fatalism. The doctrine of God's sovereignty teaches that since God is in control, our actions matter, and God's will is achieved, in part, through our actions. God ordains the ends and the means.

Fatalism is a pagan notion that says what will be will be, freedom is an illusion, and our decisions do not matter. Fatalism is a worldview in which outcomes are inevitable. This produces a spirit of resignation and passivity. Confusing sovereignty with fatalism will worsen any crisis of faith because it kills the human spirit. We are created for meaningful and intentional work. This is one important way we maintain hope and determination during a crisis of faith.

When Doubt Reveals Faith

David's persistent question ("How long?") reveals something that is encouraging during a crisis of faith. If faith is not the absence of doubt, and if active faith is fighting for its existence, then David's question shows us how doubt can reveal genuine faith.

David is asking God a question. This means David believes in God. Of course Satan also believes in God (James 2:19). David demonstrates saving faith that flows from a personal relationship with God. David feels abandoned and let down by God, which tells the reader that this is a man who is used to feeling close to God and sensing God's presence.

David wonders how long God will hide His face and conceal His counsel. He clearly believes God is personal and communicates. Carefully considered, David's statements of doubt reveal a faith that is alive and kicking.

In a crisis of faith, things often seem worse than they are in reality. Every cup is half empty. The sweetness of life is overpowered by the bitterness of struggle. We need Scripture to restore a realistic perspective. We need people who can lovingly help us connect the dots of our trials to the picture of goodness and grace that God wants us to see. We need to see the ways in which our struggle is evidence of life.

Worship in the Meantime

During a crisis of faith, it is tempting to put worship on hold and wait until the storm passes. The mistake here is in thinking that emotions must lead to actions. In fact, during a crisis of faith, this is a critical mistake.

David's psalm of personal lamentation reveals a subtle yet significant statement about surviving a crisis of faith and taking control of actions despite emotions to the contrary:

> But I have trusted in your steadfast love; my heart shall rejoice in your salvation. I will sing to the Lord, because he has dealt bountifully with me. —Psalm 13:5–6

David is reminding himself that he made a decision to trust God. What a powerful thing it is to remind yourself of your past covenant commitments. Wedding anniversaries are important for many reasons, but during years of marital hardships, they remind spouses of the promises they have made to each other.

You may have noticed that many Bibles have a section in the front where you can record the day on which you made the decision to put your faith in Jesus. We tend to remember important days. Remembering and celebrating anniversaries is one way we recommit ourselves to the things and the people that are most important.

David reminds himself that he has trusted in God. In doing so, he shows us that faith is the volitional expression of a sovereign gift. When David says, "I will sing to the Lord," he is showing the kind of resolve that survives a crisis of faith.

His resolution is not baseless stoicism. It is reasonable that David was committed to worship. He says, "I will sing to the Lord, *because* he has dealt bountifully with me" (emphasis added). God doesn't just give us commands; He gives us reasons. Adam and Eve were told not to eat of the forbidden fruit *because* it would lead to death (Genesis 2:16–17). God's people were told to honor their father and mother *so that* it would go well with them and they would live long in the land (Exodus 20:12). Commandments contain the kernels of promise. God is not like an earthly father who says, "Do it because I say so," even though He could. God gives us commandments with promises and reasons.

David taps into this logic, reason, and promise when he recalls the bounty of God's grace. God is not stingy with His mercy and His blessing. Even in his crisis of faith David has not forgotten God's track record of faithfulness. In Psalm 103:2 David says, "Bless the Lord, O my soul, and forget not all his benefits." He commands himself to worship even when he doesn't feel like worshipping.

Spiritual amnesia is forgetting God's past faithfulness in light of your current crisis. David doesn't sugarcoat life's challenges, but neither does he forget all that God has done. Calling to mind what God has done is an effective strategy for growing in faith during a crisis of faith.

Interestingly, the Bible forbids keeping a record of wrongs. In 1 Corinthians 13:5 it says that love is not resentful, which means that love does not keep a list of sins. The believer in Christ has a powerful promise and example of this kind of love from God, who casts our sins as far as the east is from the west (Psalm 103:12). This illustration communicates the absolute forgiveness of the believer in Christ. God does not hold our sins against us in Christ.

David teaches us to worship through trials. While you wait for deliverance, healing, and answers, worship in the meantime. This lesson from David is also seen in the life of the prophet Habakkuk, who lived during times of great evil and distress and yet chose an intentional life of worship:

> Though the fig tree should not blossom, nor fruit be on the vines, the produce of the olive fail and the fields yield no food, the flock be cut off from the fold and there be no herd in the stalls, yet I will rejoice in the Lord; I will take joy in the God of my salvation. God, the Lord, is my strength; he makes my feet like the deer's; he makes me tread on my high places. — Habakkuk 3:17–19

Keeping a Record of Rights

As much as we are prohibited from keeping a record of wrongs, David models the value of keeping a record of rights! Reminding yourself and others of what God has done is modeled many places in Scripture: God's people are called to remember and not forget that God led them out of slavery (Deuteronomy 6:12). The psalmist Asaph says, "In the day of trouble . . . I will remember the deeds of the Lord; yes, I will remember your wonders of old" (Psalm 77:2, 11). Peter says, "I intend always to remind you" in reference to the qualities of godliness that are fitting to the truth of the gospel (2 Peter 1:12).

When it comes to sins, we are not to keep a record, but when it comes to God's blessings, we are to always remember. The act of remembering God's past goodness during times of hardship is one way we go forward in faith. While the enemy tempts us to think God has abandoned us or has forgotten His promises, remembering God's spotless record of faithfulness combats the lies with the truth.

Biblical remembrance is more than simply recalling facts. Remembering leads to obedience. For instance, when the Bible says, "Remember the Sabbath day, to keep it holy" (Exodus 20:8), the point is not mere intellectual assent but faithful action. What we remember—the things we call to mind—affects our actions. If you remember then you obey.

No wonder the Bible says in Philippians 4:8, "Finally, brothers, whatever is true, whatever is honorable, whatever is just, whatever is pure, whatever is lovely, whatever is commendable, if there is any excellence, if there is anything worthy of praise, think about these things." Sin affects the relationship between our thoughts and actions so that there is not a perfect correspondence. In fact, Paul bemoans this fact in Romans 7, saying he often does not do in the flesh what he desires to do in the spirit. Christians are simultaneously both sinners and saints.

Thoughts and speech do not determine reality, but they influence perspective and outcomes. If you feel as though God has let you down, focusing on that fact will undoubtedly prolong a crisis of faith. On the other hand, if you choose to remember specific times when God demonstrated His faithfulness, the result is likely to be a reprieve to doubt and strengthened faith. As Shakespeare wrote so eloquently in his thirtieth sonnet, "But if the while I think on thee, dear friend, all losses are restor'd, and sorrows end." The act of remembrance is a powerful tool against unbelief.

Our individual stories have great value, but they are not as powerful as the stories of God's faithfulness in Scripture. Nothing is better than remembering the stories preserved in Scripture. Human stories are prone to exaggeration, change, embellishment, or even fabrication. We have all had the experience of remembering wrongly. Individual Christian stories can sometimes be like fishing stories where the fish gets bigger and bigger every time the story is told!

In contrast, the stories of God's faithfulness in Scripture are preserved in heaven. Remembering what God has done in Scripture is the surest footing for faith.

Hard Work and Power of Remembrance

One Christmas Eve, my wife and I put our young kids to bed and stayed up wrapping presents and putting toys together. One toy was particularly challenging: A play kitchen for our daughter. It took several hours—much longer than we had planned. Finally, early on Christmas morning, the whole thing was constructed and covered by a blanket of wrapping paper. It was time consuming and challenging, but what a joy to see my daughter on Christmas morning discovering the present. The hard work paid off.

Surviving a crisis of faith is hard work that pays off. David models the work of faith when he says in Psalm 13:5, "My heart shall rejoice in your salvation." This is the opposite of the modern secular ethos of listening to your heart or being true to yourself. David is preaching the gospel to himself and commanding his broken heart to beat with joy. In a crisis of faith, don't listen to yourself; preach to yourself.

During college, I took a road trip to Las Vegas to see a concert with friends. After the show we hit a buffet (as one does while in Vegas!) and then drove three hours to our dorm rooms, arriving early the next morning. During the last few hours of that drive, the only way I could stay awake was to roll down the windows and expose myself to the cold winter air. It was freezing, but I was awake!

No person in their right mind would willingly give in to sleep while driving. The wise person stops and rests, of course, but at the very least you do what must be done to stay awake. Because your life depends on it, you are willing to take radical steps to stay awake.

A crisis of faith is like the lull of sleep to a person who knows they must stay awake. David rouses himself, commanding himself to remember God's promises, sing, and rejoice! Like a tired person who doesn't feel like driving, David rallies himself to a state of spiritual alertness. More than physical life, eternal life depends on our alertness. As the Apostle Peters says, "Be sober-minded; be watchful. Your adversary the devil prowls around like a roaring lion, seeking someone to devour" (1 Peter 5:8).

Large mountains generate their own weather. In California, it is not uncommon to encounter unique weather patterns on the larger peaks. It can be hot and clear in the valleys, and then sudden storms will appear seemingly out of nowhere on the mountain ridges.

David demonstrates a similar principle. Strong Christians who have worked through seasons of doubt learn to generate their own weather, so to speak. Rather than waiting for preferable conditions to worship, they just worship. They pray when they don't feel like praying. They sing when they don't feel like singing. Draw near to God, and He will draw near to you (James 4:8). Emotions often follow obedience.

Jesus says in John 4:24 that true worshippers must worship in spirit and in truth. True worshippers must worship. They do not have the luxury of waiting for perfect conditions. If conditions are a prerequisite for your worship then they are, in fact, an idol. Writers write, singers sing, and worshippers worship.

David illustrates the nature of willful worship in a crisis of doubt that shows the interplay of spirit and truth that Jesus talks about. Remember the truth of what God has done. It is objective, historical, unchanging, and factual. Worship involves more than mere knowledge of facts. It involves our obedient, joyful, and loving response of faith to the truth of Scripture.

During an intellectual crisis of faith, some aspect of the truth needs assurance to our minds. We need books, lectures, discussion, logic, and arguments. At other times, paying attention to the truth, remembering God's faithfulness, and choosing to worship jump-starts the human spirit. Just as a plane cannot fly with one wing, the Christian life of worship is meant to soar on the two wings of spirit and truth.

If you know someone going through a crisis of faith, a good prayer for them is that they would remember who God is and what He has done. Pray that who they are in Christ would be central to their identity. Pray that they would recall the Bible lessons, sermons, counsel, and instruction from their youth, if they were raised in a Christian home.

Paul says something similar to his young disciple, Timothy: "I am reminded of your sincere faith, a faith that dwelt first in your grandmother Lois and your mother Eunice and now, I am sure, dwells in you as well" (2 Timothy 1:5).

In essence, Paul is saying, "Remember who you are. You are a believer, Timothy. You belong to God. Remember what your mother and grandmother taught you from the Scriptures. Let these truths guide your life."

The Ultimate Joy

David says his heart rejoices in God's salvation. More than anything else, it is the salvation of God that enables Christians to survive a crisis of faith. Take away every earthly possession, and the Christian still has God. On the worst day the biggest problem has been solved.

A crisis of faith is not good in itself, yet God uses it for good purposes. One such purpose is to strip away lesser joys in order to show us the truest, purest, and most enduring joy—the joy of a relationship with the Father by the Spirit through faith in Jesus Christ, the Savior.

To borrow from C. S. Lewis's book *The Weight of Glory*, this relationship is like a holiday at the sea, and everything else is like a child making mud pies in the gutter. There is simply no comparing the two. One is infinitely better. In *Mere Christianity* Lewis says, "If I find in myself a desire which no experience in this world can satisfy, the most probable explanation is that I was made for another world."

A crisis of faith is an instrument of grace. It strips away illusions. An intellectual crisis of faith strips away the illusion of pride and replaces it with humility. An emotional crisis of faith strips away the illusion of stoic individualism and replaces it with Christian community. A financial hardship reveals our need for daily bread. In every crisis of faith, He increases and we decrease (John 3:30)—a sweet and painful process.

Job 1:21 says God gives and takes away. Through it all, the work of faith is to bless the Lord. But why? Why would you bless God as He takes things, opportunities, people, health, and even life itself *away*? Because as He strips these things away and allows things we love to be taken away, He gives us a greater sense of His presence and salvation:

> For we know that if the tent that is our earthly home is destroyed, we have a building from God, a house not made with hands, eternal in the heavens. For in this tent we groan, longing to put on our heavenly dwelling, if indeed by putting it on we may not be found naked. —2 Corinthians 5:1–3

In his sermon titled *Indwelling Sin*, Charles Spurgeon calls self-sufficiency "Satan's net, wherein he catches men, like poor silly fish, and doth destroy them." A crisis of faith sometimes helps to free us from the entrapment of self-sufficiency and prepare us for the ultimate good of union with Christ. In a crisis of faith, you realize your intellectual, physical, relational, and fiscal limitations and weaknesses.

God uses our crisis for good, but that does not undo the inherent evil of doubt, sin, and suffering. Loss is loss. It is never good in itself. Death is the enemy. Suffering is wicked. All these things will end and have already been defeated. The snake has been mortally wounded, but it will take time for him to die.

Satan intended to kill God on the Cross, but all he did was serve the purpose of God's greater glory. So too, in human suffering, Satan intends to diminish our joy in Christ, and all he does is accentuate the glory of Christ. Our joy in Christ increases as our need of Christ increases.

Even a crisis of faith that results from our own bad decisions is drenched in mercy. The Bible says God disciplines those He loves (Hebrews 12:6). If you are under the rod of God's discipline, it is a sign that He loves you.

C. S. Lewis says in *Surprised by Joy*, "Divine punishments are also mercies." Hardships that result from bad decisions have the good effect of shaping our character and helping us to grow in wisdom. The psalmist says, "It is good for me that I was afflicted, that I might learn your statutes" (Psalm 119:71). In our failures we see more clearly our need for the law and for Jesus who fulfills its demands.

The mystery of grace in trials and the role that salvation plays in buoying faith during a time of crisis is also seen in the story of Jonah. God called the prophet Jonah to proclaim salvation to the Ninevites, a group of people generally disliked by the Israelites. Since Jonah did not want God to save the Ninevites, he ran in the opposite direction toward Tarshish (Jonah 1:3). God, the Good Shepherd, went after Jonah to ensure that the message of salvation would go to whom He chose at the time of His choosing. God used a storm to capture Jonah, who ended up in the water and then in the belly of a whale.

It is hard to imagine a direr predicament: the belly of a whale. This scene has become a metaphor for the lowest of lows. In the Bible, the whale symbolizes death itself. Jesus spends three days in the grave before rising from the dead. The whale, therefore, is a symbol of God's deliverance from sin and death. Jonah goes on to deliver the message in Nineveh, by which others are saved from sin and death. Jonah is a small preview of the deliverance that will come from the resurrection of Jesus.

Yet unlike Jesus, who never sinned and did not deserve to be in the grave, Jonah's disobedience led to his punishment. In the whale—as good as dead—Jonah prays. The words of his prayer illustrate how God uses a trial for our good and how remembrance of salvation brings joy even in the most hopeless situations:

When my life was fainting away, I remembered the Lord, and
my prayer came to you, into your holy temple. Those who pay
regard to vain idols forsake their hope of steadfast love. But I
with the voice of thanksgiving will sacrifice to you; what I have
vowed I will pay. Salvation belongs to the Lord! —Jonah 2:7–9

It is a source of comfort to know that men like David and Jonah walked
through seasons of doubt and unbelief and made it through. We not
only know *that* they made it through, but we also know *how* they made
it through their crisis of faith. They chose to remember the Lord and
think about His covenant promises.

Big wave surfing is a dangerous sport. Brave men and women ride
waves that are at least twenty feet high. When all goes well, the result
is exhilarating. However, when the surfer wipes out and goes under the
giant wave, the result is life-threatening. In such situations, surfers have
to hold their breath, endure wave after wave, and try to make it back to
the surface. Even more deadly, being under the waves is disorienting.
Sometimes the surfer underwater doesn't know what way is up.

For this reason, big wave surfers wear a brilliant device called an
inflatable vest. If a surfer is underwater, losing oxygen, disoriented, and
stuck under the waves, he or she can activate the inflatable vest and be
lifted to the surface.

In a crisis of faith, remembering that God has saved you is like an
inflatable vest. In time, it will lift you from under the waves. God's salvation will help you find the surface. When you don't even know which
way is up, living intentionally and meaningfully in light of God's covenant faithfulness will lift your soul. It will not solve all your immediate
problems, but it will provide light to make it through the darkness.

The Meaning of Happiness

During his crisis of faith as recorded in Psalm 13, David continues
to trust, rejoice, and worship (vv. 5–6). David's trust related to God's
character ("steadfast love"), his joy related to God's deliverance ("salvation"), and his worship related to God's grace ("he has dealt bountifully
with me"). Making it through a crisis of faith depends on knowing
God. For all you do not know, you do know God, even if your faith is
small, dim, and weak.

Another way God uses a crisis of faith is to teach us the *real* meaning of happiness. The world is filled with false notions of happiness, leading multitudes on a goose chase ending in hopelessness, misery, and judgment. The windmills of worldly happiness expose the folly of life apart from God.

There are basically four concepts of happiness. Most people ascribe to one of these concepts. How you define happiness will influence how you choose to live and how you define success.

1. **Happiness is pleasure**. Some ancient philosophers thought of happiness as pleasure, or the absence of pain. On this view, the good life is avoiding that which increases pain and pursuing that which increases pleasure. Since pain is the enemy of pleasure, and having pleasure is what it means to be happy, then pain is the enemy of happiness. Many people still hold this view of happiness, and as a result, spend their time in pursuit of pleasure.

   Yet so much happiness in life comes through experiences of pain. Childbirth is painful, and yet through it comes great happiness. Strenuous exercise is painful, and yet the connection between happiness and physical exertion is well established. Relationships can be painful, yet they are a necessary ingredient to happiness.

   Hebrew 12:2 says Jesus endured the Cross for the joy set before Him. Acts 16:25 describes Paul and Silas praising God in prison, undoubtedly a painful experience. The Bible (special revelation) and our experience (natural revelation) reveal the folly of the notion that happiness is pleasure.

2. **Happiness is a list**. Bucket lists are popular these days. This list of things a person hopes to do, or places they hope to go, before they die (i.e., "kick the bucket") can be innocent fun, but it can also be a wrongheaded notion of happiness.

   If happiness is checking off your list of places to go and things to do, then if you don't have the money to go on the dream vacation, you simply will not be happy. If happiness is taking a selfie in front of the Taj Mahal, and you are diagnosed with cancer and are in the hospital, then happiness is out of the question. And yet we know there are people in cancer wards and in poverty whose lives exhibit what we would call happiness. Money, opportunity, and freedom do not equal happiness.

The World Happiness Report conducts a survey of nations according to a list of things believed to equate with happiness. The list includes a country's gross domestic product, life expectancy, freedoms, and corruptions. People also rate their life, on a scale of zero to ten, to gauge happiness. The benefit of this approach is that it produces an index of happiness based on data. When a person says something like, "People in Iceland are happier than people in America," they are usually citing the World Happiness Report, and the implication is that America has something to learn from Iceland, which is undoubtedly true.

Yet the idea of such a list is flawed. Some cultures would view scoring your own life as ten out of ten as arrogant and unbecoming. In other cultures, a person whose life is a two would brag and say their life is a nine! We know from social media that people present a glorified and exaggerated version of themselves to cultivate identity to create a following. It is often called "branding yourself."

The list approach is also flawed because of what it doesn't tell you. The world happiness report doesn't tell you, for instance, that in 2013 Iceland was first in terms of people taking antidepressants.[2] In California, Marin County is an affluent area north of San Francisco with excellent schools, stunning natural beauty, amazing culture, world-class health care, and fabulous wealth. Yet in her book *The Price of Privilege*, psychologist Madeline Levine chronicles the high levels of addiction, depression, anxiety, and other psychological problems among teenagers of affluent families in this area.

A list of factors related to happiness is culturally biased and prone to miss clear symptoms of unhappiness. People can check off boxes that should indicate happiness and yet be miserable. Or, as comedian Louis C. K. said on the late-night talk show *Conan*, "Everything is amazing right now and nobody's happy."

3. Happiness is desire fulfillment. A third option is that

[2] OECD (2015), *Health at a Glance 2015: OECD Indicators,* OECD Publishing, Paris. *http://dx.doi.org/10.1787/health_glance-2015-en.*

happiness is the ability to fulfill desires. If you can marry the person you desire, stay single if you desire, or work the job you desire, then you should be happy. Happiness on this view is about fulfilling your desires.

Clearly there are problems with this view. People who are addicted to drugs regularly fulfill their desire for drugs, and yet we would not call them happy people. Serial killers have a desire to kill and fulfill that desire, and yet we would not call them happy people.

4. **Happiness is knowing God.** Christianity offers an alternative theory of happiness; happiness is knowing God. By "knowing" we mean a saving relationship. Happiness is being a child of God the Father, having Christ as brother, the Spirit as helper, and God's people as family. On this view of happiness, you may never achieve your human dreams of happiness. Your earthly desires may go unfulfilled, and yet you may experience unspeakable joy. Your pain may exceed your pleasure, but if you know God you will not be a miserable soul.

David could sing, rejoice, and write a song about worship—even while in the trenches of a crisis of faith—because he knew God. A life lived knowing God often comes with physical pleasure, fulfilled desires, and the ability to check off personal goals and dreams. But don't confuse these things with happiness. Contrary to popular opinion, David proves you can lose these things without losing true happiness.

The Unavoidable Question and the Defiance of Faith

The twentieth-century French philosopher Albert Camus says in his book *The Myth of Sisyphus* that one day in life the inevitable question, "Why?" arises. For some people, the why occurs during college. For others, it surfaces during a time of personal hardship. At some point, we start asking why. Why do bad things happen to good people? Why should I believe in God? Why is Christianity true and other religions wrong? If there is no God, then what (if anything) can give meaning to life?

Camus, like his fellow existential nihilist, Jean-Paul Sartre, was committed to the view that there is no God and life is random and meaningless. They believed that life was irrational, but humans papered over this haunting fact with nostalgic acts, finding unity in scientific and religious myths. Their answer was to embrace the absurd, which meant embracing the present over the past or the future. Living without regard for eternity is the real act of defiance against the meaninglessness of life. The absurd, therefore, serves the role of god and provides meaning. Meaninglessness is the bread, and absurdity the wine, of high-modern individualism.

Embracing life as meaningless usually resulted in despair and anxiety. Martin Heidegger regarded anxiety as the source of human experience. In a life without meaning, humans work because they are anxious about money, love because they are anxious about loneliness, and care for themselves because they are anxious about death. In religion, humans go to church because they are anxious about hell and judgment.

Here is the point. David does not shy away from the hard questions. He knows that apart from God life has no ultimate meaning. Why has God forgotten me? Why am I suffering? Why is God hiding? Why are my enemies winning?

The Bibles teaches us both how to question and how to answer. The questions have *ultimate* answers but not always *immediate* answers. There is no reason to think that David knew the immediate reasons for his crisis of faith, but he clearly knew the ultimate reasons why he should keep believing.

Genuine faith is defiant against uncertainty. It chooses to worship, trust, and believe even when there are no easy answers. Behind this kind of determined faith is a keen and powerful grasp of ultimate answers: God doesn't change, God saves, and God is gracious. David never gets an answer (that we know of) to his questions, but his faith is restored by focusing on who God is and what God has done.

Chapter 7

Gideon: Far from a Hero

By this point several things should be clear. First, it is common for believers to go through a crisis of faith. Even heroes of faith go through crises of faith. Second, the presence of doubt does not mean the absence of faith. Third, faith is the refusal to panic. Fourth, biblical faith is a dimmer switch—sometimes it is bright and other times it is dim.

The Bible is not silent about Christians who doubt, and we should not be silent about our own doubt. When (not *if*, but *when*) you go through a crisis of faith, commit yourself to the acts of faith even as you wait for your faith to recover. Whatever else is going wrong, the resurrection proves that your biggest problem has already been solved. Your best life is yet to come. The fact of salvation infuses meaning to work and relationships, however hard they might be at the moment. The weight of life is a glorious struggle.

One believer who struggled with persistent doubt is Gideon, a hero of faith mentioned in Hebrews 11, along with David, Samuel, and the prophets. You may know the sanitized Gideon of flannelgraphs and children's storybook Bibles. This Gideon has been airbrushed. He gallantly led a small army with no real weapons in a stunning victory against a much larger enemy, the Midianites. Gideon is often presented as a one-dimensional archetype symbolizing confidence, resourcefulness (a kind of biblical MacGyver of eighties television fame), and persistence.

The real Gideon is more complicated, textured, and interesting. His story is one of faith plagued by near constant doubt and second-guessing God. Once again, the point is not to glorify doubt but rather to marvel that God accomplishes His purposes despite our often weak-kneed faith. Gideon makes it through his crisis of faith the same way anyone does—by God's grace.

Mighty Man of Valor

The story of Gideon unfolds in three chapters in the Book of Judges. In chapter·six the Bible introduces Gideon against the backdrop of Israel's idolatry. The Midianites oppressed Israel as God's instrument of judgment. Yet God mercifully provided a judge named Gideon. Judges in the Old Testament did not sit in courthouses, wear robes, or bang gavels; they were regional civil and military leaders who led God's people amidst religious diversity.

One day, while beating wheat inside the winepress, Gideon was called into ministry. You don't have to be a farmer to know that a winepress is for pressing wine, not beating out wheat! Gideon is hiding his wheat from the Midianites (Judges 6:11).

Out of nowhere the Angel of the Lord appeared and said, "The Lord is with you, O mighty man of valor" (v. 12). The Lord has a sense of humor! Gideon hid from the very people God was going to use him to defeat. The point is not that God sees something in Gideon he does not yet see in himself. The point is God is going to use a weak man to accomplish His purposes in order to display His strength (2 Corinthians 4:7). Our fear does not limit God's power.

Who was the Angel of the Lord? His identity is revealed when he said to Gideon, "The Lord is with you" (Judges 6:12). The Angel of the Lord was the Lord Himself, a preincarnate appearance of Jesus (Judges 13). Gideon was skeptical. He responded by asking, "If the Lord is with us, why then has all this happened to us?" (Judges 6:13).

Gideon was too busy asking questions that had already been answered to see the amazing gift of God's presence before his very eyes. God had already sent a prophet to tell Israel why they were suffering. God had not abandoned them or been unfaithful to His promises. Israel suffered because of their disobedience (v. 10).

God's promise to Gideon was that He would use Gideon to save Israel. It would be God's presence and God's power at work in Gideon (v. 16). God's promise was backed by a spotless record of past faithfulness. He reminds Gideon that he led the Israelites out of Egypt (v. 13). It is always God's faithfulness in the past that justifies our obedience in the present.

But Gideon, like all human beings, persists in unbelief. He accused God of forsaking his people (v. 13). God told Gideon not to be afraid. He specifically said, "You shall not die" (v. 23). But when God instructed Gideon to tear down the places of false worship, Gideon did it at night "because he was too afraid" (v. 27).

Unreasonable Demands

Gideon's unbelief was most prominently displayed in the now famous incident of the fleece. Remember God said He would save Israel. He told Gideon he would not die, and Gideon had seen the Lord face to face (v. 22). What more evidence did he need?

All the miracles and evidence were not enough for Gideon. In what was an astounding incident of human unbelief and divine patience, Gideon asks God for a sign. In essence, he tells God His word was not enough. Gideon wanted proof. Specifically, he lays out fabric made of wool (a fleece) and instructs God to make it wet by morning, and then Gideon would obey.

The next morning the fleece is wet. So wet, in fact, that Gideon has to wring it out, like a bath towel soaked through. But so great is Gideon's unbelief that he asks God for another sign. This time, he wants to put the fleece out overnight, and he wants the fleece to be dry and the ground around it to be wet (vv. 36–40). God does exactly as Gideon asked. Amazing grace, indeed.

This passage most certainly *does not support* the practice of asking God for signs. Such a practice goes directly against the teaching of Jesus, who said, "An evil and adulterous generation seeks for a sign" (Matthew 16:4). In the Gospel of Luke, Jesus described unbelievers as those who "kept seeking from him a sign" (Luke 11:16).

Gideon's fleecing incident is an example of what *not to do* in your relationship with God. You may be wondering, why is it wrong? After all, God created humans with rational faculties. Isn't it true, as we have observed, that God is gracious to give evidence for His existence and for the validity of His Word? Indeed, this is all true.

However, there is a difference between leaning on the evidence God gives and asking for more evidence, as though what He has provided is insufficient. The doctrine of the sufficiency of Scripture is contained in such places as 2 Peter 1:3, where it says that God has granted to his church "all things that pertain to life and godliness" through the knowledge of Christ in Scripture. The prophetic word (v. 19) is the "precious and very great promises" (v. 4) contained in Scripture (v. 20).

Asking God for more evidence in your crisis of faith will only worsen your unbelief for two reasons. First, it blames God for unbelief, as though God has not done enough. As though the resurrection is not evidence enough. As though the thousands of miracles recorded and preserved in Scripture are not enough. You must decide; are they enough? Read and reread and find that they are enough. Peter says that it is better to have the Word than to experience miracles for yourself (v. 19).

The second reason "fleecing" will worsen your unbelief has to do with the nature of unbelief. One sign will not be enough. Gideon asks for a second sign, a different sign, a better sign. If God proves Himself by healing you, then what trick must He perform next? Must He provide you with the winning lottery numbers? Must He become a genie in a bottle? If this were the case, He would hardly be a God worth believing. He would be the clay, and you would be the potter. In this sense, asking for a sign is falling prey to the original sin—the desire to be God.

Root sins, such as pride, lead a person to ask for more evidence when enough evidence has already been provided. Demanding signs is often an ungrateful heart masquerading as reason. Rather than thanking God for all the evidence He has graciously provided, we demand more. Like a spoiled child who opens up all the Christmas presents under the tree and then looks to her loving father and says, "Is that all you got for me?"

Unbridled reason is a spoiled brat who can only say, "More." It is never enough. Why? Because reason is not intended to be separated from revelation, and here I am referring to the Bible. When human reason is guided by Scripture it is a beautiful tool. When human reason is separated from revelation it becomes a traitor to the self. Reason apart from revelation is an enemy, it is not to be trusted, and it leads to absurdity.

Reason by itself leads to absurdity, meaninglessness, and irrationality. Existentialist philosopher Franz Kafka presented a powerful picture of the absurdity of reason apart from revelation in the parable he relayed of a man fishing in his own bathtub. Concerned, a visitor tactfully asked, "Are they biting?" to which the man replied, "Of course not, you fool, since this is a bathtub!"

Something is absurd if it makes no sense. Christian musician Chris Rice had a song titled "Smell the Color Nine" that perfectly captures the idea of absurdity. Trying to live life apart from God is like trying to smell the color nine.

Reason without revelation is like a rocket without a guidance system. The power of thrust—intended for good—dooms the unguided rocket to a fiery disaster. So too is reason without revelation. The spoiled impulse of depravity is to ask God for that which He has already provided. The staggering presumption of unbelief stands in contrast to the tender mercies of God in the story of Gideon and the fleece.

Reason is also like a gun. In good hands it serves good purposes, and in evil hands it serves evil purposes. As an instrument of unbelief, reason has an insatiable appetite for evidence but is never satisfied. Jesus makes this point when He tells the story of the rich man and Lazarus, as recorded in Luke 16:19–31.

A rich man dies and goes to hell while Lazarus, a poor beggar, dies and goes to heaven. The rich man begs Abraham to send Lazarus to his family and warn them so they too do not end up in the place of torment (v. 28). Abraham tells the rich man his family has Scripture (i.e., Moses and the prophets), and that should be enough. The man insists Lazarus goes and warns his family, to which Abraham replies, "If they do not hear Moses and the Prophets, neither will they be convinced if someone should rise from the dead" (v. 31).

Addiction—in whatever form it takes—always demands more. It is never satisfied. Reason without revelation is merely a form of addiction—to self, autonomy, and life without God. A crisis of faith is often experienced at the crossroads of trust and demand. A person must choose. God mercifully aids His people in making the decision they would otherwise not be willing to make. Trust is often the fruitful result of a long and painful process of humiliation. God commanded Gideon to break down the altar to his idols, but God had to strip Gideon of his pride. Pride is always the greater idol.

A Humiliating Victory

A crisis of faith is sometimes a process of going backward in order to go forward. We spoke of such paradoxes in previous chapters. In Gideon's case, the victory is humiliation.

Gideon had more than thirty thousand men in his army. God refused to allow Gideon to go into battle with that many men. God said to Gideon, "The people with you are too many for me to give the Midianites into their hand, lest Israel boast over me, saying, 'My own hand has saved me'" (Judges 7:2). If Gideon had experienced a victory with thirty thousand men, it would have been Gideon's victory. He would have seen himself as the savior, and God loves us too much to ever let us mistake ourselves for the Savior.

John Calvin said in *The Institutes of the Christian Religion* that the human mind is a perpetual forge of idols. Modern society ups the ante, combining the idol-making tendencies of human depravity with the self-absorption and self-promotion of tech to mass-produce little saviors and messiahs. Whereas God showed Gideon he was not the Savior through a process of humiliation, modern man appears almost wholly obsessed with the self as brand; *imago selfie*. The sin of pride is not new, but modern tech enables pride in an entirely new way.

We now have armies of little Gideons with their thirty thousand followers. In their hand they hold the tool of self-promotion, and by their hand they believe themselves capable of great victory, even changing the world. Yet eventually it becomes clear that the emperors have no clothes—high profile ex-evangelical figures who publicly repudiate their faith, such as Bart Campolo, Derek Webb, Joshua Harris, and Marty Sampson (to name a few). The process of losing faith as the result of a crisis of faith has been called deconversion.

These defections produce sadness, anger, disappointment, and confusion. Yet there is nothing new under the sun. The early church had its Diotrephes, who "likes to put himself first" (3 John 1:9) and went on to reject the authority of the apostles. How timely the biblical warnings that "not many of you should become teachers" (James 3:1) and, "Whoever causes one of these little ones who believe in me to sin, it would be better for him if a great millstone were hung around his neck and he were thrown into the sea" (Mark 9:42).

Jesus had thirty years of instruction before going public. Paul and the apostles had three years of training. Perhaps the church is guilty of looking to people who have learned how to be public Christians before they have learned to be private Christians. Premature exaltation runs a predictable route: Private doubt becomes a public declaration of unbelief. Everything secret will come to light (Luke 8:17). How many of these men will return to the faith? I hope they all do.

I would have counseled these men to heed the advice of Blaise Pascal from *Pensées*—go to church, read the Bible, and put yourself in the paths of grace. Live faithful and quiet lives. Ask God to give you faith.

Heeding Pascal's advice takes humility, patience, and other virtues that are counterproductive to self-promotion and evangelical superstardom.

God loves Gideon enough to take away his followers in order to train him to become a follower, however frail and broken a follower he proves himself to be. Gideon went to battle with only 1 percent of his troops. When they blew the trumpets, lit the torches, and broke the jars (as God had instructed) the enemy soldiers were panicked and confused. In darkness and chaos, "The Lord set every man's sword against his comrade and against all the army" (Judges 7:22). Clearly the battle belonged to the Lord. God saved Israel. There can be no doubt that Gideon was not the hero of the story. Deliverance came through humiliation, and strength came through weakness.

Gideon was not an overcomer. He seems not to have learned from his initial doubts and fears. He went fearfully into battle (vv. 10–11). He displayed pride and arrogance when he told his men to shout "For the Lord and for Gideon" (v. 18).[1] *And for Gideon*? Gideon had the

---

[1] This can be taken innocently enough, but Dan Block also observed that the narrator may have intended some ambiguity, given subsequent comments in chapter eight. Daniel Block, "*Judges and Ruth*," The New American Commentary, Volume 6 (Broadman & Holman Publishers, 1999), 282.

good sense to refuse the offer to be king, telling Israel that God had delivered them (Judges 8:3) and that God would rule over them (v. 23). But then Gideon became a sort of *de facto* king (v. 29)[2] who takes for himself many wives with whom he has seventy sons (v. 30).

In addition to Gideon's lust for power and lust for women he returned to idolatry. Judges 8:22–29 describes how Gideon collected gold and constructed the same kind of idol he tore down in Judges 6:27. He tore down the idol by night in chapter six and then constructed a new form of idol in broad daylight, so to speak, putting the idol in his city, where "all Israel whored after it and it became a snare to Gideon and to his family" (Judges 8:27). Faith takes one step forward, and doubt takes two steps back.

The Bible says Gideon dies at a "good old age" (v. 32). So what do we make of Gideon? He was a humbled victor and a doubt-filled believer. The Bible describes Gideon, and other heroes of the faith, as being "made strong out of weakness" (Hebrews 11:34). Strength in weakness is not absurd, but it is a paradox.

Strong in Weakness

In many ways, a crisis of faith is the process of God breaking idols. In his *Large Catechism*, Martin Luther defines idolatry as "whatever your heart clings to and confides in." Worship has the effect of conforming the one worshipping to that which is worshipped. Worship the living God, and you grow to be like Him. Worship idols that look alive but are dead (i.e., eyes that cannot see and ears that cannot hear), and you grow to be like them. As the psalmist writes:

> Their idols are silver and gold, the work of human hands. They have mouths, but do not speak; eyes, but do not see. They have ears, but do not hear; noses, but do not smell. They have hands, but do not feel; feet, but do not walk; and they do not make a sound in their throat. Those who make them become like them; so do all who trust in them. —Psalm 115:4–8

---

[2] Ibid., 300. "To live in his own house" seems to imply something more than simply residing in one's own home. It likely carries the implication of a kind of rule, which is supported by the context.

A crisis of faith helps you to identify idols. The thing you think you cannot live without, or without which you cannot be happy, or the thing that defines you, is probably an idol. *Syncretism* is a big word that simply means to combine religions. At Sinai, the Israelites tried to worship a golden calf and Yahweh (Exodus 32:1–6). Combining true worship and false worship is syncretism.

The form of syncretism most popular in American Christianity seems to be the blending of soft-core Christianity with what professor of psychology Paul Vitz calls the "cult of self-worship." Soft-core Christianity has the basic features of Christian orthodoxy, minus any strong emphasis on sacrifice, suffering, repentance, discipleship, or holiness. The cult of self-worship, on the other hand, features variations of self-realization (one part Carl Jung and one part Abraham Maslow) minus the disclaimer that "Jungian psychotherapy is . . . a *Heilsweg*, in the twofold sense of the German word: a way of healing and a way of salvation."[3]

Soft-core Christianity and the cult of self-worship syncretize to fashion a god in man's image. This god lives for our glory and wants man to be fulfilled, self-aware, whole, well-adjusted, and balanced. A person who bows to the golden calf of self-worship while calling it gospel or Jesus will endure a crisis of faith when they discover that the real God of the Bible is more concerned with holiness than worldly happiness. God ends up being a cosmic disappointment when He doesn't grant wishes or move mountains. When people realize the "self" is deceptive and elusive (Jeremiah 17:9), not like a butterfly, which is easily caught and pinned down, they will feel as though God were rather disappointing.

All of this will be experienced as a crisis of faith. In reality, God is breaking idols. He is destroying the idol of self. He is paring down the army of human pride and self-exaltation to reveal core truths. Fallen man cannot save himself. The answers do not lie within. Idols turn men into zombies. The most dangerous idol is the one staring at you in the mirror.

A crisis is a fork in the road. By it God lovingly separates His children from the idols their hearts have created. The process is painful, and the cost of spiritual victory is often humiliation. A crisis of faith does not create or destroy faith, but it does reveal the object of worship and the presence of idols.

---

[3] Jolande Jacobi, *The Psychology of C. G. Jung*, English edition (Yale University Press, 1973), 60.

A financial crisis of faith can expose idolatry about money and security. A health scare can expose the idolatry of youth, leisure, and comfort. A marital scare can expose idolatry about identity and image. Such experiences are painful to go through, and yet how sweet the fellowship with Christ and His people when altars of idol worship have been torn down.

The Apostle Paul puts it this way:

> But we have this treasure in jars of clay, to show that the surpassing power belongs to God and not to us. We are afflicted in every way, but not crushed; perplexed, but not driven to despair; persecuted, but not forsaken; struck down, but not destroyed; always carrying in the body the death of Jesus, so that the life of Jesus may also be manifested in our bodies. For we who live are always being given over to death for Jesus' sake, so that the life of Jesus also may be manifested in our mortal flesh. So death is at work in us, but life in you. —2 Corinthians 4:7–12

Worship Is Warfare

A crisis of faith also serves the purpose of revealing the spiritual battle of everyday life. One minute Gideon was working on the family farm, and the next minute Jesus was talking to him about going to war. Gideon's crisis was a calling: a call to war. Gideon's physical war illustrates the cosmic battle raging around us continuously between the absolute rule and reign of God and the limited rule and reign of Satan.

God is sovereign, and Jesus is victorious. On the Cross Jesus said, "It is finished" (John 19:30). Nevertheless, Christians live between the times. The fall and the Cross are in the past, while restoration and glorification are in the future. The kingdom is not of this earth, but through the local church and in the lives of the elect there are brilliant flashes of the kingdom that foreshadow what is to come when Jesus returns.

In the meantime, the church is at war. We know a day is coming when people from every nation, tribe, and language will gather around the throne and worship the Lamb (Revelation 7:9). There is also a beast, who has limited authority over every nation, tribe, people, and language (Revelation 13:5–7). Authority is the battleground.

It is common for modern Christians to spend their days ignoring the reality of spiritual conflict. A life crisis provides insight and clarity. In one sense you feel as though you are in a daze. In another sense, you feel sober and awake to the reality of good and evil, right and wrong, justice and injustice, life and death: an avalanche of reality.

Working through the crisis of faith leads to a decision. *What do I believe? Whose authority do I trust? Is Jesus alive, or is He dead?* You must ask and answer these questions. They become to the believer a kind of mantra in a crisis of faith. So many things are unknown, and yet not everything is a mystery. It has been said but bears repeating: focus on what you know to be true.

A crisis of faith is a crisis of authority. Satan is called the god of this world (2 Corinthians 4:4), the prince of the power of the air (Ephesians 2:2), and the ruler of this world (John 14:30). God is sovereign, and yet He has allowed Satan to have limited authority.

No wonder Peter says, "Be sober-minded; be watchful. Your adversary the devil prowls around like a roaring lion, seeking someone to devour" (1 Peter 5:8). A crisis of faith demands a decision in regard to authority—whether to follow the lies of Satan and the empty philosophies of the world in self-worship or accept the authority of Jesus who rose from the dead.[4]

When Jesus gave His disciples the Great Commission He began by saying, "All authority in heaven and on earth has been given to me" (Matthew 28:18). Each person must decide for themselves, commit themselves, and regularly recommit themselves to the absolute authority of Christ. Gideon says, "The Lord will rule over you" (Judges 8:23). However poorly Gideon lived out this truth, it was a truth he believed nonetheless.

Something will rule over you. A crisis of faith is a crisis of authority. Something happens, and you begin to question whether to trust Jesus or yourself, Jesus or society, Jesus or trends, etc. It is not always the case that one must choose; natural law says there are elements of grace and truth in all aspects of human life. Yet given the enemy's earthly authority, cunning, and intent on devouring (if possible) even

---

[4] I am indebted to my friend Dr. Ben Arbour who, in conversations, reminded me of the verses pertaining to the relative authority of Satan and helped to make the connection between worship and authority.

the elect, there are daily points of decision where one must choose (Matthew 24:24).

Choosing is warfare. It is the battle of the mind, thought, will, and affection. It is the battle over words. Every yes and every no is a declaration of authority. Choosing to live and believe is a declaration of war against absurdity, meaninglessness, and idolatry. In this war there is no neutrality. Everyone is religious.

In a crisis of faith one must decide to trust the absolute authority of Jesus: Worship is a posture of submission and humility before God. Choosing to worship is the way that God's people have always waged war. The Ark of the Covenant in the Old Testament was not only a symbol of God's presence. God led Israel into battle by it.

David says God is enthroned on the praises of His people (Psalm 22:3). The kingdom of light spreads into the kingdom of darkness not by political activism, force, or coercion but by praise and obedience. As John Piper says in his book *Let the Nations Be Glad!*, "Mission exists because worship doesn't."

Paul tells believers to put on the whole armor (literally, the complete armor) of God in order to stand against the schemes of the devil (Ephesians 6:10–20). The Greek word for *schemes* is *methodeia*, the root of the English word method. Satan has his methods—deceit, accusation, distraction, temptation, to name a few.

Against these doubt-invoking methods the Apostle Paul commends to believers a strategy for standing strong. It is a timeless defense that needs no improvement. It is simple and straightforward; a child can follow this battle plan, and scholars can ponder its brilliance.

The truth of the gospel is a belt that keeps everything else together. The righteousness of Christ is a breastplate that protects your heart. The gospel of peace enables you to stand. The Christian faith is a shield that extinguishes all the flaming darts of the evil one—*all of them*. Salvation is a helmet, the Bible is a sword, and prayer is a weapon (Ephesians 6:10–20).

If a person doesn't have the armor provided by God, he attempts to construct his own armor, just as Adam in the Garden of Eden constructed his own covering of fig leaves. There are various ways humans try to cover themselves apart from God. Image is a weapon. *Project* the "self" in order to *protect* the "self." Parents sometimes hide behind their children whom they send into the world as proxies of themselves. Our phones can be our shields we hide behind to keep from having to interact. Music, television, books, drugs, and alcohol are all weapons of modern secular humanism.

In a crisis of faith, a believer realizes the futility of these alternative weapons against the schemes and lies of Satan. Only real light can dispel real darkness. God takes away what cannot save us in order to save us. He tears us down to build us up, a painful and necessary process.

Ex-Evangelicals

A growing number of people who have left the Christian faith identify as ex-evangelical. When doubt wins and the light is off, there never was the light of conversion. Everyone was fooled.

The Bible teaches two things that must be affirmed, however great the tension. First, the Bible teaches that a genuinely saved person cannot lose their salvation. Jesus says, "I shall lose none of all those he has given me" (John 6:39 NIV); "He who began a good work in you will bring it to completion at the day of Jesus Christ" (Philippians 1:6); the Holy Spirit is a deposit guaranteeing our inheritance (Ephesians 1:13–14); and nothing shall separate the believer from the love of God in Christ Jesus (Romans 8:31–39).

The doctrine of eternal security is rooted in divine election. Before the foundation of the world, God chose believers to be adopted (Ephesians 1:4) as His children by faith. Nothing can revoke God's elective grace (Romans 11:29). In a crisis of faith, being reminded that God chose you, and will never abandon you, is like a warm fire on a cold night. You will make it through the cold night if you stay close to the fire.

It is true that genuine saints persevere in the faith. But there is another truth, more like a sobering bucket of cold water than a warm fire on a cold night. This second truth is that Christians must guard themselves, commit themselves, remain awake and alert, and not drift away from the truth. This second truth is that the Bible warns Christians against falling away because many professing Christians do fall away. Jesus says few find the narrow road to eternal life, but *many* the wide path to destruction. Jesus says that on the day of judgment *many* are turned away (Mathew 7:12–23).

The sobering bucket of cold water is the contrast between the words *few* and *many* in places like Matthew 7. *Few* implies rarity, in comparison with the commonness of the word *many*. It is rare for a professing believer to endure and common for them to give up.

Cheap Grace in a Crisis of Faith

People give up in different ways. In Matthew 7, people do not give up professing faith (i.e., "Lord, Lord"), but they do give up actually following Jesus. The doctrine of perseverance is not merely that people will endure in their profession of faith but also in their work of faith. Professing faith but not seeking to live it out in obedience is what Dietrich Bonhoeffer called "cheap grace" in his famous book *The Cost of Discipleship*.

Cheap grace produces a culture of doubt. It is faith that is heard but not seen and is therefore untrustworthy. Cheap grace is confusing. It is all smoke and no fire. Children who grow up in homes filled with cheap grace hear about a God who forgives from parents who keep a record of wrongs. This is more than, "I do the very thing I hate" (Romans 7:15); it is the evil calm of spiritual complacency. A conspiracy of cheap grace.

Confession and repentance build trust. Holiness is loving. Cheap grace is easy come and easy go. It is the stuff of deconversion. Cheap grace builds a house of cards on a foundation of sand.

A crisis of faith will rescue you from cheap grace. David says, "It is good for me that I was afflicted, that I might learn your statutes" (Psalm 119:71). Cheap grace says obedience is optional. Biblical grace trains us to renounce ungodliness and worldly passions and live self-controlled, upright, and godly lives in the present age (Titus 2:12).

In a crisis of faith, cheap grace is not your friend. Grace that coddles unbelief and allows for faith on individual terms is not saving grace. Saving grace commands faith, is merciful to those in doubt, and enables broken people to be strong in the Lord (Ephesians 6:10).

Gideon shows the sinfulness of sin and the great mercy of God. The Bible does not gloss over Gideon's many faults and failures, but there is a silver lining. In the postscript to Gideon's life, it says:

As soon as Gideon died, the people of Israel turned again and whored after the Baals and made Baal-berith their god. And the people of Israel did not remember the Lord their God, who had delivered them from the hand of all their enemies on every side, and they did not show steadfast love to the family of Jerubbaal (that is, Gideon) in return for all the good that he had done to Israel. —Judges 8:33–35

Amazingly, Gideon's many faults and failure did not entirely eclipse his faith. Note that it was *after* Gideon died that the people of Israel turned again to shameless idolatry and disobedience. Gideon had been used by God to stem the tide of faithlessness. In context, Gideon was (by comparison) a man of faith, however weak and inconsistent.

Gideon is not the hero, but neither is he the villain. He is proof that God uses fallen people to accomplish His purposes. God uses doubting believers. Somehow in the divine economy of grace a doubting person plus God's elective grace equals a legacy of faith.

This is good news. God used Moses (a bad speaker . . . and murderer), Jeremiah (only a youth), and Isaiah (a man of unclean lips). Gideon's doubt-filled life was not wasted. God whittled down Gideon's army to show the unworthiness of man and the great mercy of God. Perhaps no man in the Old Testament so proves the point of God's persistent and gracious love more so than Gideon.

Perhaps he is a kind hero after all, only a different kind of hero from the one we were taught as kids. He is not the hero who shows against-all-odds faith and resilient courage. He is a hero in the sense he proved what this book has argued: believers doubt, God is bigger than our doubt, genuine faith is persistent, and doubt does not have the final say. In the end, faith wins.

Gideon is an antihero. He lacked the typical great-making characteristics usually celebrated in heroes. Even through his doubt he maintained a desire for God to be known and obeyed.

He may have limped across the finish line, but he made it across. Gideon is counted alongside a king like David and a prophet like Samuel, men who possessed the assurance of things hoped for, the conviction of things not seen (Hebrews 11:1).

Gideon and the Gospel

Gideon is mentioned in Judges and Hebrews but nowhere else in the

Bible. He is a minor character. His story starts and ends with doubt. His life is comprised of a thin slice of reluctant faith sandwiched by thick doubt.

But the real legacy of Gideon is his victory over the Midianites with only three hundred men, torches, vases, and trumpets—an absurd victory indeed. God saved His people in a way no one could have seen coming.

Gideon foreshadows a greater judge (Acts 17:31). One who is a light that shines in the darkness (John 1:5). A king whose final salvation will come with the sound of trumpets (1 Thessalonians 4:16). The treasure of the knowledge of Jesus in the gospel is possessed in jars of clay, to show the power belongs to God (2 Corinthians 4:7).

God displays His power in our weakness. When we are weak He is strong (2 Corinthians 12:10). He is the hero.

Chapter 8

Jeremiah: Send Someone Else

In Anthony Doerr's Pulitzer Prize-winning novel *All the Light We Cannot See*, Daniel LeBlanc hides a priceless jewel called the Sea of Flames during the 1940 Nazi invasion of France. He and his blind daughter Marie-Laure escape Paris and hide within the walled city of Saint-Malo, a coastal town on the English Channel where Daniel's uncle lives.

All the Light We Cannot See is filled with intrigue and disguise. Banned radios are disguised inside oatmeal boxes. Safes are disguised as children's toys. Fake jewels are disguised as real ones.

In this chapter we will explore how disobedience can be disguised as doubt. Saying, "I don't know if I believe," can sometimes mean, "I don't know if I want to obey." In such cases, unbelief is a convenient excuse for doing what we want rather than what God commands. When we play this game, sin leads to greater doubt, which in turn leads to greater sin.

Not every crisis of faith is a pretext for disobedience. While all doubt is disobedience in the sense that we are called to believe, some instances of doubt are caused by events outside our control: spiritual abuse, sickness, abandonment, etc. Other instances of doubt are intellectual in nature: unanswered questions that cause us to doubt the Christian faith. Such crises of faith require compassion, patience, counseling, and thoughtful dialogue in the context of a local church.

But there are times when doubt is a thinly veiled attempt to justify disobedience, and objections are a pretext for ignoring God. To see the nature of this deceit, let us consider the story of when God called the prophet Jeremiah.

Only a Youth

In Jeremiah 1:4–8, it says:

> Now the word of the Lord came to me, saying, "Before I formed you in the womb I knew you, and before you were born I consecrated you; I appointed you a prophet to the nations." Then I said, "Ah, Lord God! Behold, I do not know how to speak, for I am only a youth." But the Lord said to me, "Do not say, 'I am only a youth'; for to all to whom I send you, you shall go, and whatever I command you, you shall speak. Do not be afraid of them, for I am with you to deliver you, declares the Lord."

The scene begins with a startling revelation. Before Jeremiah was conceived, God chose him for a noble yet dangerous job. God set Jeremiah apart to be a prophet to the nations (i.e., the world). While not everyone is chosen for this particular ministry assignment, everyone in Christ shares in this testimony of elective grace. If you have saving faith, then you too are chosen (Ephesians 1:4).

In response to God's declaration of eternal affection and dignified purpose, Jeremiah shrugged: "Ah, Lord God!" This effectively indicated a thanks-but-no-thanks reply. Jeremiah's alibi was his age. He reasoned he was too young to fulfill the job requirements.

The reader sees through the pretense. Jeremiah offers a reasoned response to God when reason does not support his unbelief. *It never does.* If an all-powerful God exists, and if God has an unchanging will, perfect love, and perfect power, then it *stands to reason* that this same God can enable a young man to speak.

Jeremiah has an excuse; it's just not a good one.

God's response to Jeremiah supports this conclusion, "Do not say 'I am only a youth.'" Jeremiah uses a Hebrew word (*naar*), meaning either a boy or a young man. The exact age is not important. Jeremiah is using his age as an excuse for disobedience.

On the surface, his excuse makes sense. Think about it. If you were going to choose someone to speak to the world on behalf of God, would you choose any boy or young man you know? Wouldn't you select a polished communicator? Someone with experience in public speaking? I would too.

But God chooses the weak to shame the strong (1 Corinthians 1:27). As with Gideon, his intent is to show off His power, not ours. Nothing against polished and experienced communicators! God uses them, but he doesn't *need* them.

Jeremiah's doubt doesn't hold up precisely because God is God. His presence by the Spirit is all the power Jeremiah needs to fulfill the mission. Jeremiah is focused on his age and (by inference) his knowledge and ability. Jeremiah's doubt is the result of self-focus. Feeding self-focus prolongs doubt. God graciously redirects Jeremiah's focus. The issue is not what Jeremiah can do but what God can do through Jeremiah.

Here is the point: Doubt looks inward, but faith looks upward. Remember that a believer is called to preach to himself, not listen to himself. The pew is not the psychoanalyst's couch. It is a place of receiving truth outside oneself, not answers from within. A crisis of faith magnifies personal weakness and limitations, and at the same time, God's absolute unlimited character. He is all we are not, and to the believer, this is a great comfort in a crisis of faith.

German pastor and theologian Dietrich Bonhoeffer was imprisoned, and later executed, for his participation with an organization that conspired to kill Adolf Hitler. At Christmas in 1943, he helped to write a prayer that was distributed to the other prisoners. The prayer he wrote, while in a desperate situation, highlighted the faith-building contrast between God and man:

> O God,
> Early in the morning do I cry unto thee.
> Help me to pray,
> And to think only of thee.
> I cannot pray alone.
> In me there is darkness,
> But with thee there is light.
> I am lonely, but thou leavest me not.

I am feeble in heart, but thou leavest me not.
I am restless, but with thee there is peace.
In me there is bitterness, but with thee there is patience;
Thy ways are past understanding, but
Thou knowest the way for me.

Grace for Today

It's easy to empathize with Jeremiah. Even with the best theology, it is hard to imagine yourself doing something you have never done. Future grace—the stuff we need from God to face tomorrow's challenges with obedient faith—is abstract. We believe in it as one believes in a concept. Future grace is a precious promise from God, but we live in the present, and therefore present doubt seems real in a way that future grace does not.

Jeremiah had never been God's global spokesman. A cursory reading of the prophets makes it clear prophets were not welcome and often persecuted. God calling Jeremiah was the Old Testament version of Jesus calling His disciples to take up their cross. Stephen says to the religious leaders who killed Jesus, "Which of the prophets did your fathers not persecute?" (Acts 7:52).

Being a prophet was hard work. Jeremiah was called to demolish in order that God might build (Jeremiah 1:10). Jeremiah was warned that the nations would fight against him but not prevail against him (v. 19). Now you understand why Jeremiah didn't want the job!

It is hard to imagine yourself doing something you've never done. Hard to welcome divine assignments that involve pain and discomfort. You may be fearful that God's will for your life may involve permitting some particular form of suffering such as cancer, the death of a child, abuse, divorce, or bankruptcy. The very thought of these especially hard forms of suffering may cause you to grow weak in faith. You may think, "If that were to happen, I don't know how I could continue to believe."

The promise of future grace is like the promise of a future resurrection when all bodies will be raised back to life. I know God will raise dead bodies, but I cannot imagine what that will be like, let alone what it will feel like to be resurrected. That event is in the future, and I am in the present. There is a gap between my faith and my imagination. I cannot fault myself for the limits of my experience and imagination because it is how God made me, but I can choose to believe in a future resurrection even if I cannot imagine what it will be like.

We must circle back to this point: *God commands belief.* Faith is the assurance of things hoped for, the conviction of things not seen (Hebrews 11:1). And so, in regard to the resurrection, I believe Jesus rose from the dead. Moreover, I believe everyone who places their trust in Jesus will be raised like Jesus to eternal life. *We* will not stay in the grave because *He* did not stay in the grave.

But these things are in the future, and I am in the present. I cannot imagine dying, let alone coming back to life in a new body on a new heaven and new earth. I believe these things will take place, but I do not understand how they will take place. It is hard to imagine yourself doing something you've never done.

God gives us grace for today and the promise of grace for tomorrow. Whatever hardship you fear most—whatever pain or suffering you cannot imagine yourself going through in the future—is not what you are going through *today*. God is giving you grace for the present.

Today God is giving you grace. He is taking care of you right now. Therefore what reason do you have for doubting He will provide you the grace you need for tomorrow's challenges? Whatever tomorrow holds, whatever unimaginable darkness may be just around the corner, God has promised to be with you and have sufficient grace to see you through.

Grace is like the manna (i.e., bread) that God used to feed the Israelites in the wilderness. The Israelites were commanded to eat manna but forbidden to store it, except for the Sabbath (Exodus 16:23–24). Like manna, grace is God's provision for today. It is new every morning, and it is only for today (Lamentations 3:22–23). As we sing in the old hymn, "Great Is Thy Faithfulness," God gives us "strength for today and bright hope for tomorrow."

In her book *The Hiding Place,* Corrie ten Boom tells the story of fearing her father's death and the unimaginable pain she would experience at his passing. She cried out "I need you! You can't die! You can't!" Her father's response illustrates the promise of daily grace:

> Father sat down on the edge of the narrow bed. "Corrie," he began gently, "when you and I go to Amsterdam—when do I

give you your ticket?"

I sniffled a few times, considering this.

"Why, just before we get on the train."

"Exactly. And our wise Father in heaven knows when we're going to need things, too. Don't run out ahead of Him, Corrie. When the time comes that some of us will have to die, you will look into your heart and find the strength you need—just in time."

What great advice: Don't run out ahead of God. Take a crisis of faith one day at a time. There is sufficient grace for today, and God will give you grace for tomorrow's challenges, whatever may come.

Jeremiah knew God provided for Moses, another leader who struggled to speak. His challenge then, and our challenge now, is to apply the lessons of faith and remember that the same God who was with Moses and Jeremiah abides inside of us. He will have sufficient grace for our trials when we need it, but not beforehand.

A Crisis of Imagination

A crisis of faith is not always about what happened in the past or what is happening in the present. A crisis of faith can be rooted in the fear of what *might* happen, fear of the unknown. Have you ever found yourself thinking about some terrifying scenario? Your sympathetic nervous system causes your body to sweat and your heart to race. A runaway imagination can be spiritually, emotionally, and physically debilitating.

Imagination is a gift. When used properly, the mind combines truth with creativity. It enables planning and ideation. Humans are made in God's image. God is creative, and so are humans. God's creativity is on display in such things as mountain ranges, human diversity, and solar systems. Human creativity is on display in such things as architecture, literature, and entrepreneurship. Human creativity is an argument for God's existence.

But sin leads imagination astray. Sin imagines the future through a lens of fear and doubt rather than love and hope. It assumes the worst. Imagination in service to hope leads to faith. Imagination in service to fear leads to doubt.

A realistic person expects hardships and disappointments in this life. Pain and suffering are inevitable. Yet there is a difference between realism and pessimism. Realism has hope, and pessimism does not. Christianity requires that we approach the world realistically; there is great pain and suffering, but there is also great hope.

A person who envisions the worst apart from the hope of the gospel is a slave to their imagination. It can be a helpful exercise to allow yourself to assume the worst. What if the worst-case scenario came true? What then? Would God be with you? Would God be good? Would God be for you?

Such a thought experiment shines light into the darkness of human imagination. It is like a child, turning on the lights, looking under the bed, and finding that the monster they feared is not there. It is true that terrible things happen. It is also true that God is making all things new (Revelation 21:5).

God is with His people in hospital rooms, business meetings, and on battlefields. His grace is sufficient at all times and in all places. His power is made perfect in weakness (2 Corinthians 12:9). When life is most bitter, Christ is most sweet.

How do you regain control of your thoughts when you are captive to a runaway imagination? Scripture is the emergency brake. Focus your attention on all God is rather than all you are not. Remind yourself of what you know. Preach to yourself.

Remember that God's grace is a renewable resource. Use today's grace to strengthen today's faith. Every day in which the worst *does not happen* is a day for you to prepare for that day on which it does. Choose to prepare rather than fear.

Using daily grace for crisis preparation is a matter of walking in the biblical disciplines such as daily time in the Word, confession, repentance, service, evangelism, church membership, and thanksgiving. These timeless disciplines are how Christians prepare themselves for suffering and how they make it through suffering.

Godly Routines as Crisis Preparation

Practicing Christian disciplines cultivates routines of faith that will sustain you in a crisis. The word *routine* often has negative connotations.

For some people, it brings to mind that which is emotionless, boring, and ritualistic.

In fact, routines are like the frame of a house. You may change the color of the paint on the walls, or the flooring on the foundation, but you are not likely to mess with the foundation beneath the floor, or the studs behind the walls. The structure keeps the housing standing.

Routines are the structure to life. Like bones to the human body, everything else hangs upon your routines. The word *routine* comes from the word route, which brings to mind a road. Routines are the well-worn paths of your daily life.

Although we often use the word *routine* interchangeably with the word *habit*, there is an important difference between the two. Habits are what you do, and routines are how you do what you do. Routines make habits stick.

A routine is an intentional set of actions that you do on a regular basis in a regular way. Think about your life. An example of your routine may be the way you make breakfast or the sequence of things that you do when you come home from work.

Everyone has routines, but not everyone has *godly* routines that reflect biblical priorities. For instance, does your morning routine reflect the priority of time with God? Do your workplace routines reflect concern for your coworkers, or are you only concerned with yourself? Do your evening routines build community and health, or are they isolating and harmful?

Godly routines are the floor you stand on in a crisis of faith. They are the walls to shelter you from the storm. If you lack them, you will be hard-pressed to endure a crisis. The time to stormproof your house is before a storm, not during it.

Sadly, many Christians give little thought to their routines. In a crisis of faith, they discover that a life consumed with entertainment, distractions, worldliness, and self-centeredness is a house poorly built. Remember, the best time to plant a tree is twenty years ago, but the second best time to plant a tree is today.

Staying in shape is easier than getting in shape. However, if you are not in shape, you can change your routines and get in shape. It is hard work, but by God's grace, it is possible. If you are reading this book and fearing some possible future event, transfer the energy of fear into an energy of preparation. Join a church and serve. Get a Bible and read it. Make some friends who love Jesus and have been living for Him seriously and hang out with them, learn from them, and learn their routines. Make wise decisions with your money and your body.

If you choose to re-routine your life, the energy of godly preparation will produce unexpected joy. I suspect you will find yourself thinking about the challenges of today rather than the potential challenges of tomorrow. Maintaining godly routines today will take your full energy, so there will be little energy left for fretting over tomorrow. There is no time to worry when your time is spent living, loving, serving, and growing. Today has enough trouble of its own (Matthew 6:34).

No More Excuses

We learn from Jeremiah that focusing on self leads to a crisis of faith, and the way out of such a crisis of faith is to focus on God. We have seen that doubts are often tied to worry about the future. We have seen that daily grace and godly routines are important ways to battle runaway imaginations.

Now we must confront the thorny issue of excuses. All of us are guilty of being like the lazy people in the parable of the great banquet who "all alike began to make excuses" (Luke 14:18). God gives the banquet, and we give excuses.

This is an ancient problem. Back in the Garden of Eden, Adam immediately blamed Eve (and God) for his sin. Adam ate the forbidden fruit, but rather than confessing, he blamed God for giving him a wife who had given him the fruit to eat (Genesis 3:12). Thus began a daily and universal cycle of humans blaming others for their own sin.

We are all prone to making excuses. Jeremiah uses his youth as an excuse for not obeying God. Many of us made the same excuse when we were young, telling ourselves we would wait until we were older to obey God's commands. Of course it is never wise to delay obedience.

Excuses are the worst kind of lies. An excuse is a lie to oneself. Telling a lie to another person requires you at least know the truth and then decide to somehow obscure the truth. When we make excuses, we engage in self-deceit. Regarding self-deception, A. W. Tozer writes in *Man: The Dwelling Place of God*:

When a man is deceived by another he is deceived against his will. He is contending against an adversary and is temporarily the victim of the other's guile. Since he expects his foe to take advantage of him he is watchful and quick to suspect trickery. Under such circumstances it is possible to be deceived sometimes and for a short while, but because the victim is resisting he may break out of the trap and escape before too long. With the self-deceived it is quite different. He is his own enemy and is working a fraud upon himself. He wants to believe the lie and is psychologically conditioned to do so. He does not resist the deceit but collaborates with it against himself. There is no struggle, because the victim surrenders before the fight begins. He enjoys being deceived.

The Bible says that if you think you're something when you are nothing, you deceive yourself (Galatians 6:3). Self-deception is the unwise act of comparing yourself with yourself (2 Corinthians 10:12). Rather than weighing his thoughts and beliefs against the truth of Scripture, a self-deceived man is satisfied with whatever seems right in his own eyes (Judges 17:6).

Jesus says the truth will set you free (John 8:32). Tozer says in his book *Jesus, Our Man in Glory*, "We are too nice! We are too tolerant! We are too anxious to be popular! We are too quick to make excuses for sin in its many forms!"

Excuses often mask themselves as intellectual objections. As Paul says:

> For the wrath of God is revealed from heaven against all ungodliness and unrighteousness of men, who by their unrighteousness suppress the truth. For what can be known about God is plain to them, because God has shown it to them. For his invisible attributes, namely, his eternal power and divine nature, have been clearly perceived, ever since the creation of the world, in the things that have been made. *So they are without excuse.* —Romans 1:18–20 (emphasis added)

The words "without excuse" come from the Greek word *anapologétos*, which literally means without (*an*) defense (*apologetos*). Christian apologetics (*apologia*) comes from this same word, meaning to defend the faith. While the Bible claims there are many ways to defend faith in God (1 Peter 3:15 and Acts 1:3), belief that there is no God or that there is not enough evidence to justify belief in God is indefensible.

Intellectual excuses are not the only kind of excuse. We previously identified intellectual and experiential doubts. Similarly, there are also excuses that are intellectual in nature, and excuses that are personal (i.e., related to experience, failure, disappointments, and grief).

What is your excuse for not fully trusting God? Jeremiah's excuse was his age. God responds to Jeremiah by saying, "Do not say 'I am only a youth.'" God is gracious, but He does not believe the lies we tell ourselves.

It's not that Jeremiah was wrong about his age. In a crisis of faith, you can have the right information and the wrong perspective. Jeremiah was young and inexperienced! But when God calls, He provides.

It turns out God was right! Jeremiah wasn't too young. By God's grace, he was an effective minister to God's people. Jeremiah would have missed out on the privilege of obedience had God not lovingly exposed and removed his excuse.

Excuses steal, kill, and destroy. They keep us from enjoying life in Christ to the fullest. A crisis of faith is a perfect opportunity for God and His people to help expose, confess, and remove excuses. In a crisis of faith, explanations are your friend, and excuses are your enemy.

Self-Control as a Weapon Against Doubt

At this point, we've discussed many of the weapons that comprise the Christian's arsenal against unbelief, including Scripture, resolve, community, evidence, prayer, and remembrance. These are powerful weapons. Depending on the crisis and the circumstances, one of these (or all of them) may be deployed to combat unbelief and strengthen faith. Combine them with confession, repentance, and dogged refusal to accept excuses, and every genuine Christian will (by God's grace) make it through a crisis of faith (Romans 8:28–30).[1]

---

[1] I do not say every *professing* Christian but rather every *genuine* Christian. For evidence of genuine conversion, read the Book of 1 John.

God has given us weapons that preserve our faith in the battle against unbelief. One such weapon that has the power to neutralize a crisis of faith and undo its debilitating effects is self-control.

More than apologetic books, arguments, and evidence, in a crisis of faith you need self-control, which is a component of the fruit of the Spirit in Galatians 5:22–23. In every situation where a believer exhibits self-control there is evidence of God's existence and saving presence.

When Paul instructs older women to teach younger women and older men to teach younger men, only one thing is mentioned to both groups: self-control (Titus 2:4–7). It is the cornerstone of biblical virtue and godly living: thou shalt control thyself.

Wisdom is the application of truth to everyday life. To do this, one must know the truth and then possess by the Spirit the ability to be self-controlled. A self-controlled person is functioning properly. God's will for your life is self-control (1 Thessalonians 4:3).

The philosopher Plato argued that the soul is rightly governed by the mind, not by the heart or the stomach. Each of these three aspects of human nature has a corresponding virtue—reason for the mind, courage for the heart, and self-control for the stomach. A person who is out of order and malfunctioning is ruled by his urges and appetite. The mind, he argues, must direct the passions and the appetite, and not the other way around.

Plato knew intuitively what modern man seems to have forgotten: self-control is essential for a rightly ordered life, and a rightly ordered life is essential for happiness.

Internally, self-control is about guarding your thoughts, keeping a rein on your emotions, and scrutinizing your thoughts. Externally, self-control is about physical restraint, literally managing the actions of your body. Interestingly, James says of the tongue:

> Look at the ships also: though they are so large and are driven by strong winds, they are guided by a very small rudder wherever the will of the pilot directs. So also the tongue is a small member, yet it boasts of great things. How great a forest is set ablaze by such a small fire! And the tongue is a fire, a world of unrighteousness. The tongue is set among our members,

staining the whole body, setting on fire the entire course of life, and set on fire by hell. For every kind of beast and bird, of reptile and sea creature, can be tamed and has been tamed by mankind, but no human being can tame the tongue. It is a restless evil, full of deadly poison. —James 3:4–8

Think of the tongue like the point of contact between the immaterial self (the soul) and the material self (the body). These two things, which together constitute the self in its fullest sense, interact mysteriously when thoughts turn into words. Breath forced through teeth and tongue is shaped into sound, which, by the ingenuity of human creativeness, map to arbitrary symbols for the external world that we call words. There is mystery, power, and serious consequences to human speech. Communication is a privilege that requires serious thought and control. The tongue is a fire, a world of evil.

A crisis of faith often becomes a crisis of control. Let us be candid: in seasons of doubt and unbelief, people do stupid things. They let their tongue off the leash. A private and personal season of doubt spreads like wildfire. Families are ruined, careers implode, irreversible damage is done—all for a lack of self-control owed to a crisis of faith.

Hopefully you are beginning to see the tremendous value of the words of Martyn Lloyd-Jones we considered way back in chapter 1 when he says that faith is the refusal to panic. It will take self-control to make it through a crisis of faith. Specifically, there are three areas of life in which self-control is key to surviving doubt with your faith intact.

First, self-control is needed to regulate thoughts. In a crisis of faith, we tend to paint in broad strokes, lacking precision to capture what is true. For instance, in a crisis of faith that is triggered by relational turmoil, it is easy to overgeneralize: "Everyone is fake," "The church is full of hypocrites," "Leaders are two-faced," etc. Most of us have dealt with fake people, hypocrites, and unqualified leaders, and we have all been guilty of these same sins. But these generalized statements commit what logicians call the fallacy of hasty generalization. Many people in church are genuine, and many churches have godly and qualified leaders.

Be on guard for lies. Replace statements like, "I can't do this," with, "I need God's help to do this." A subtle shift in thinking brings truth and hope. For example, rather than saying, "I don't have any friends," say, "I need to develop closer relationships." Loneliness breeds despair, but the truth is that friendship requires work and effort. The first statement reflects helplessness, while the second reflects hope and implies a reasonable action step.

In a crisis of faith, we sulk and nurse our wounds with lies. Seeking counsel with friends who only reinforce these uncharitable thoughts worsens the crisis and causes doubt to spiral out of control. It takes self-control and godly friends to help us catch these lies. Without making excuses for sin, self-control looks for the good in others, especially brothers and sisters in Christ. It takes self-control to love as God commands.

Second, self-control is needed to regulate actions. When people panic, they make bad choices. For instance, in a crisis of faith associated with a difficult marriage, leaving your spouse can look like an easy fix. In reality, a crisis of faith usually clouds judgment and impairs wise decision-making. A crisis of faith is usually the wrong time to make life-changing decisions. Acting on biblical principle and preestablished convictions is one thing, but basing your decisions solely on emotion, impulse, or whim will almost always make things worse and lead to serious regret.

Solomon says, "There is a way that seems right to a man, but its end is the way to death" (Proverbs 14:12). He also says, "The way of a fool is right in his own eyes, but a wise man listens to advice" (Proverbs 12:15). A crisis of faith produces a kind of tunnel vision; you can only see the problem, what you don't know, and what is wrong. Scripture, godly friends, and wise counsel provide much-needed perspective to shape information.

Think about drunk driving. Driving drunk is wrong for many reasons, but physiologically, being drunk simply makes it hard to drive! Alcohol impairs vision, decision-making, and motor skills. Sobriety restores these faculties and enables safe driving.

A crisis of faith dulls the senses and distorts vision. People in a crisis of faith often feel as though they are in a spiritual fog. Given time, prayer, and wise actions, the fog will lift, and sobriety will return. At that point, the believer is once again capable of seeing clearly in order to make serious decisions. A drunk person should wait to drive.

A Christian inebriated by doubt and crisis should postpone major decisions.

Third, self-control is needed in regard to your emotions. It is a common myth that emotions are always to be expressed and trusted. In *Hamlet*, Polonius says, "This above all—to thine own self be true." In his book *Stand Firm: Resisting the Self-Improvement Craze*, Danish professor of psychology Svend Brinkmann says, "Analyzing and finding yourself are two of the most all-pervasive concepts in contemporary culture."

People love themselves. Self-love is so basic to human existence that Jesus uses it as a starting point for considering how we should care for others. He says love others as you love yourself (Mark 12:31). The command is to love others. The assumption is that you already love yourself. Loving self is *natural*. Loving others is *supernatural*.

Contrary to Shakespeare, the biblical principle is not to follow thyself but *to thine own self be controlled*. The key to self-knowledge is in Scripture, not in a randomized personality test or any other pseudo-scientific quackery. Whatever personality is (and we don't know) and however many types there may be (anyone's guess), Scripture offers a beautifully simple analysis of the self.

You are one of a kind. There is no type for you—no color, acronym, animal type, etc. Your emotions and actions are influenced by your life stage, circumstances, health, and any number of other factors. Each individual is a mystery, known only to God. Chasing the self is like chasing a shadow.

It is doubtful you will truly ever know yourself in this life, but God expects you to control yourself in this life. In a crisis of faith, it helps greatly to shift from self-knowledge and self-discovery to self-control. Why do I fear the things I fear? Perhaps I will never know. But I can choose by God's grace to act according to faith and not according to my fears. Godliness requires self-control, not self-discovery.

Paradoxically, when we focus on God we learn more about ourselves. When we lose ourselves we find ourselves. In serving others we find true greatness (Mark 10:43). Chasing the windmill of self is a fool's errand, it is counterproductive in a crisis of faith and is not a biblical path to the recovery of faith.

In a crisis of faith, look to Jesus. He is the author and perfecter of your faith (Hebrews 12:1–2). Christ, in turn, commands us to be self-controlled (Titus 2:12). Grace requires self-control, not self-introspection. The more we look within, the more we will stumble.

Listen to Him

When Jesus was baptized, the Father said, "This is my beloved Son, with whom I am well pleased" (Matthew 3:17). When Jesus was transfigured before Peter, James, and John, the Father said "This is my beloved Son; listen to him" (Mark 9:7). Moses and Elijah were standing with Jesus at His transfiguration (vv. 1–8) because the Law and prophets point to the identity and authority of Jesus. In a crisis of faith, our affections and allegiances are bombarded by competing voices. Train your ears to hear the voice of Jesus in the Word.

Jeremiah's crisis of faith ends when the focus shifts from his excuses to God's presence and provision:

Do not say, "I am only a youth"; for to all to whom I send you, you shall go, and whatever I command you, you shall speak. Do not be afraid of them, for I am with you to deliver you, declares the Lord. —Jeremiah 1:7–8

The voices of unbelief add to the cacophony of doubt and idolatry. God's voice brings clarity, peace, and faith. Excuses disappear in the light of God's presence and grace. If God is with you, then you can trust and obey.

In the Bible, there is a story of three faithful Hebrew men who are thrown into a fire for trusting God and choosing to obey his commands. Shadrach, Meshach, and Abednego chose to die rather than worship King Nebuchadnezzar's false gods. These men did not know whether God would save them from the fire or deliver them from it, but they were prepared to die for their faith (Daniel 3:8–23).

Nebuchadnezzar was furious. He made the fire so hot that his men who threw Shadrach, Meshach, and Abednego into the fire were themselves killed by the heat. Meanwhile, the Hebrews who were thrown into the fire were unharmed:

Then King Nebuchadnezzar was astonished and rose up in haste. He declared to his counselors, "Did we not cast three men bound into the fire?" They answered and said to the king, "True, O king." He answered and said, "But I see four men unbound, walking in the midst of the fire, and they are not hurt; and the appearance of the fourth is like a son of the gods." vv. 24–25

Jesus was with Shadrach, Meshach, and Abednego in the fire. He saved them from death, and if you have trusted in Jesus as your Lord and Savior, He will save you from death and judgment. He will not spare you from hardships and trials, but He will be with you, and He will preserve you.

You can trust God. He will give you the grace you need for all of life's hardships. Let His power and presence quiet your excuses.

Practical Steps for Dealing with Doubt

In 2008, then White House Chief of Staff Rahm Emanuel said in an interview with the *Wall Street Journal*, "You never want a serious crisis to go to waste." In his book *Crisis and Leviathan*, Robert Higgs talks about how a crisis results in shifts of power. Emmanuel and Higgs agree that a crisis is an opportunity for strategic realignment. Strategic realignment is a restructure to better achieve a mission.

A crisis of faith presents a similar opportunity. When life is going well, you fall into patterns and rhythms that may or may not be healthy. During a crisis of faith, you are forced to evaluate your beliefs, activities, priorities, and relationships.

Doubt is not intrinsically good. Something is intrinsically good if it is good in itself. For instance, God is intrinsically good. Doubt, on the other hand, is good in a different sense. It has instrumental goodness, which means it is good because of what God *accomplishes through it* in the lives of those who believe in Him.

From the stories we explored in this book, we saw the role of doubt in the unfolding story of redemption. As we come to an end, we will explore the different ways a crisis of faith starts (i.e., the most common on-ramps to doubt). Then we will see different ways a crisis of faith ends (i.e., the most common off-ramps to doubt), followed by practical steps for dealing with doubt in order to survive a crisis of faith. These practical steps will enable you to leverage your season of doubt to achieve strategic realignment: restructuring your life to better accomplish the mission of trusting God and living for His glory.

Four Common Ways a Crisis of Faith Starts

The previous chapters established four common on-ramps to a crisis of faith; sin, suffering, scholarship, and surprise. Each on-ramp has unique challenges and potential solutions. As with any generalization, your experience of doubt may be different, or it may be some combination of these four. Nevertheless, understanding the common ways a crisis of faith starts is helpful to developing a strategy for dealing with doubt.

First, sin is a common on-ramp to a crisis of faith. The most common sin, as we have seen, is failing to trust God. There are many well-known Bible verses about faith, such as Proverbs 3:5, which says, "Trust in the Lord with all your heart." But trusting God is more than a single verse; it's really the point of the Bible. The Bible is a true story about a God who rescues lost people who trust Him. In every crisis of faith, there is an element of human failure to trust God.

Other sins can play a part in a crisis of faith. Willful disobedience to God will lead to spiritual anxiety. Knowing what is right and choosing what is wrong will eventually lead to a crisis of faith. Sin has a desensitizing effect to the presence and purposes of God. To the extent that you pursue the momentary pleasures of sin, you will not feel the abiding pleasures of union with God in Christ.

Losing your joy does not mean you have lost your salvation. Your salvation and right standing with God is entirely and irrevocably based on the merit of Christ. However, you will not experience the joy and security of that relationship while walking in sin. Godly sorrow is like a fire alarm. It notifies us of danger and prompts actions (confession and repentance).

If *godly sorrow* is a fire alarm, then *worldly sorrow* is a false alarm (2 Corinthians 7:10). Worldly sorrow alerts us to the presence of sin but does not lead to action (i.e., confession and repentance). The persistent lack of Spirit-led change suggests that you have not experienced a saving relationship with God (Colossians 1:22–23). This truth motivates both a genuine fear of being self-deceived about salvation and zeal for good works (Titus 2:11–14).

Sin dulls our senses and keeps us from enjoying fellowship with God. By analogy, consider a person who does not eat foods with processed sugar (e.g., candy, ice cream, soda, etc.). If that person were to eat a banana or an apple, they would better enjoy the natural sweetness of the fruit.

On the other hand, a person who regularly eats processed sweets is unlikely to enjoy the natural sweetness of fruit. Their taste buds have been dulled to natural sweetness by the cloying sweetness of processed sugar.

Sin, like processed sugar, offers momentary pleasure. It dulls our senses (to true goodness and beauty) while creating both addiction and regret. Since no man can serve two masters (Matthew 6:24), willful disobedience will make a person feel torn, wrenched, and divided. Sin produces a crisis of faith.

Sin makes man his own enemy. Peter says that fleshly lusts wage war against the soul (1 Peter 2:11). The biblical concept of integrity refers to a kind of union between right belief (orthodoxy) and practice (orthopraxy). In the space between belief and action is the shame of hypocrisy: "Wretched man that I am! Who will deliver me from this body of death?" (Romans 7:24).

David was a man whose sin brought him to crisis. In addition to his infamous adultery with Bathsheba and murder of her husband Uriah, David had many wives and concubines (2 Samuel 3), failed to discipline his children (1 Kings 1:6), and ignored wise counsel on multiple occasions (e.g., 2 Samuel 24:2 -15). David is a man whose sin contributed to his crises and led others to experience disease, destruction, and death.

Suffering is another common cause of a crisis of faith. We see this in the story of John the Baptist, whose time in prison led him to second-guess the identity of Jesus. For Gideon, it was the humiliation of being dominated by a foreign power that led him to doubt God.

These men experienced varying types and degrees of suffering. The issue is not the amount (how much) or type (what kind) of suffering you endure but rather the experience of suffering. Philosophers and theologians refer to the relationship between suffering and doubt as the problem of evil. In his book *The Cross of Christ*, John Stott said, "The fact of suffering undoubtedly constitutes the single greatest challenge to the Christian faith."

It takes effort and intentionality to maintain faith in the midst of suffering. In one sense, it is hard to keep believing when you are suffering. In another sense, it is harder to stop believing. If you stop believing because of evil and suffering, your suffering almost always continues. You still experience evil.

Yet if you stop believing in God, you cannot explain why evil is evil or why suffering is wrong. In addition to this intellectual dilemma, you lose hope and the promise of reward at the end of suffering. Without God, suffering becomes a tunnel with no light at the end.

In addition to sin and suffering, a crisis of faith is sometimes the result of scholarship: an academic or intellectual challenge to Christian faith. These challenges may come from external sources (e.g., book, teacher, etc.) or from internal questions or problems that remain unanswered.

What principles guide a believer during a crisis of scholarship? First, scholarship is good, but it is not God. What is regarded as scholarly is largely dependent on academic consensus. Academic consensus is often wrong and prone to change. If you must choose between being perceived as scholarly or being faithful to Christ, do as Norman Geisler and William Roach say in their book *Defending Inerrancy*, "Always choose lordship over scholarship."

Second, in a crisis of scholarship, keep ultimate questions in mind. You may not know the age of the universe, but you know the universe exists and it has not always existed. Big-bang cosmology says the universe has a beginning. How did the universe begin? It must have been caused by something other than the universe. Darwinism cannot explain the origin of an intricate and information-rich universe. The cause of the universe must be intelligent in order to account for the information in the universe. The cause of the universe must also be supremely powerful in order to account for the energy in the universe.

Many of us have smart homes—homes designed with complex and information-rich systems. By analogy, the universe is a smart home designed by God specifically for humans (Psalm 104:19). An intelligent cause powerful enough to generate all the energy and information contained in the cosmos is the kind of personal creator revealed in the person of Jesus Christ. The Creator wants to be known, not merely known about.

Go back to ultimate questions. You may be struggling with a moral issue related to gender or sexuality. You may be concerned that traditional Christianity has it wrong about sexuality. But if we are wrong, then whether or not you realize it, you believe in moral absolutes, also called moral objectivity (i.e., right and wrong).

Moral objectivity holds that there are moral facts in the universe, and like mathematical or historical facts, moral facts are not culturally relative (i.e., they do not change). Now ask yourself this question: What kind of origin story could account for a universe in which there are moral facts? It would seem to be that only a Moral Lawgiver (i.e., God) could account for the existence of moral facts, and it would seem that human outrage over moral injustice would only make sense if human beings were made in God's image.

Humans are made in God's image, and yet we have made a terrible mess of things. In the incarnation, the Son of God becomes human in order to save humanity. The gospel is a rescue story where God, the Creator and Moral Lawgiver, pays the price for sin.

In a crisis of faith brought on by scholarship, remember what you know. The existence of the cosmos and moral laws are like dots. When you connect these dots with other dots (i.e., such things as the resurrection, personal experience, and beauty) they form a picture. It is a picture of a world created by a God who intends for us to know that He exists.

God intends for you to connect the dots. His Spirit enables you to believe in the picture reality projects. He wants to be known and wants a relationship with you, provided you will believe.

A crisis of faith can start with sin, suffering, scholarship, or it can come as a complete surprise. We see this in the case of Elijah. One moment he is on Mount Carmel experiencing victory over the prophets of Baal, and the next moment he is running in fear for his life. A crisis of faith can hit without warning and without reason. (See also Job 2:3).

Upon further reflection, you may discover underlying issues that contribute to a sudden crisis of faith. For instance, it is common for people to experience what psychologists call seasonal depression. Some people experience seasonal depression during winter, when days are shorter, sunshine decreases, and temperatures cool. In addition, holidays can be stressful. For some, holidays are a reminder of deceased loved ones, family trauma, or an acute sense of the passing of time.

All this to say that sometimes an unexplained crisis of faith is connected to underlying issues. It is wise to consult with a physician in order to identify other potential factors or rule out complications.

A mysterious crisis of faith may also result from spiritual warfare. In such cases, doubt is brought on not by personal sin, suffering, or scholarship but by demonic attack. Satan is real, and what the Bible says about him is true. Therefore it stands to reason that a crisis of faith could be an instance of spiritual attack. Satan is the father of lies (John 8:44) whose goal is to sow seeds of doubt in order to produce a harvest of unbelief.

In order to stand firm against spiritual attack, you will need the whole armor of God (Ephesians 6:11–18). God's armor is comprised of hearing His word, prayer, and Christian community.[1] The local church is like a heavily armored tank where believers find both protection and ammunition to battle unbelief and advance the gospel.

Just because you don't know where a crisis of faith comes from doesn't mean you are helpless. *You are never helpless in a crisis of faith.* There is always fight left in faith. God equips you with everything you need to make it through a crisis of faith (2 Peter 1:3). Because of God's indwelling Spirit and His abiding Word, you are never alone, and you are never helpless.

A crisis of faith can result from sin, suffering, scholarship, or be a total surprise. In general, these are ways a crisis of faith starts. In the next section we will consider how a crisis of faith ends.

Five Common Ways a Crisis of Faith Ends

A crisis of faith commonly ends in one of five ways: action, crisis, time, mystery, or death. As with the common ways a crisis of faith starts, the common ways a crisis of faith stops are not always distinct, and you may experience overlap. Nevertheless, there is wisdom in considering these different off-ramps to doubt.

---

[1] The pronouns in the armor of God passage are plural, indicating that the whole armor of God is intended for God's people in community, not in isolation. So in Ephesians 6:11, when it says, "You may be able to stand against the schemes of the devil," the second person usage means everyone, as a body of faith.

First, a crisis of faith can end as the result of intentional and deliberate action—specific steps you take to addresses the underlying issues associated with your crisis of faith. Examples of deliberate action include researching a theological issue, repenting of an underlying sin issue, getting counseling, or joining a Bible-believing church to connect with gospel community.

Deliberate action can end a crisis of faith. Decide to do certain things, execute those decisions, and repeat this process. Take control of yourself (self-control) during a crisis of faith. Own your responsibilities. God uses intentional and deliberate action to accomplish His will for us and to help us see the light of the gospel at the end of every tunnel.

Genuine faith must be thick-skinned, willful, and assertive. We have seen from Jeremiah the need to avoid excuses ("Do not say 'I am only a youth'"), from John the need to remember what we know ("Tell John what you see and hear"), and from David the need to worship even when trials continue ("I will sing to the Lord").

Deliberate action to end a crisis of faith almost always involves a group of people helping you fight for faith. This may be a small group at church, friends who share your commitments to Scripture and can help you think through your questions and doubts, or a family member with whom you regularly process spiritual things. As Christians we are born again into a family of faith (i.e., the church). That family is part of the means by which we grow in our faith, and at times, stay in the faith.

Deliberate action can include reading a book, listening to a sermon, or having lunch with a more mature Christian in order to gain wisdom and instruction. Call it mentorship, discipleship, coaching, or something else: *find someone* who has been through what you're going through, and learn from them. Solicit advice and direction from your church leaders.

Whatever the cause of your crisis of faith, you are never alone, and you are never helpless. Regardless of how you feel, the truth is that God is with you (Hebrews 13:5*b*), God is for you (Romans 8:31), and God has equipped you (2 Peter 1:3). You possess His Spirit, His Word, and His people. You have what you need.

Deliberate action can end a crisis of faith. However, in some cases, a crisis of faith only ends when a life crisis emerges. You heard that right. Sometimes it can take a crisis to get out of a crisis. One crisis gets you into a crisis of faith, and another gets you out.

Second, a financial crisis may put you into a season of doubt, and a health crisis may usher you into a season of strengthened faith. The death of a loved one may put you into a crisis of faith while a marriage crisis may rekindle your faith. One crisis can take you down while another crisis can bring you back up again.

The Bible confirms this paradox. James says trials should be considered as "all joy" because the testing of faith leads to spiritual maturity (James 1:2–4). In *The Problem of Pain*, C. S. Lewis says pain is God's megaphone: "Pain insists upon being attended to. God whispers to us in our pleasures, speaks in our conscience, but shouts in our pain: it is His megaphone to rouse a deaf world."

Lewis had indeed experienced great pain. He was seriously injured during World War I, and then later in life, his wife died of cancer. He endured both physical and mental pain. Lewis knew pain was God's way of keeping us from mistaking this world for home, He continues in *The Problem of Pain*, "Our Father refreshes us on the journey with some pleasant inns, but will not encourage us to mistake them for home."

Pain is God's megaphone. You can grow comfortable in life and begin to think more about sports, social media, or entertainment than you do about God. In this state of spiritual drift, you take God for granted and begin to think you don't really need Him. Thankfully, God gets our attention through the megaphone of pain.

In times of suffering, things like sports, social media, or entertainment can offer no comfort for your soul. Pain illuminates your need for God. It can take a life crisis to end a crisis of faith.

Third, a crisis of faith sometimes ends only after a long period of time. In such cases, it is not specific actions, such as researching an apologetic issue or academic concern, nor is it the resolution of some instance of suffering. A crisis of faith can dissipate slowly. Over time, doubt subsides and faith returns.

The challenge in such situations is the often-glacial pace of recovery. In addition to the general advice given thus far, the key to surviving a long-term crisis of faith is patience, persistence, and perspective. Patience is trusting God to do what He alone can do *as you do* all that is within your power to do.

Persistence is the lifeline of faith during a long-term crisis of faith—doing what is right over and over again.

For instance, a hard marriage can result in a crisis of faith. Marriage can be hard for long periods of time. During those long stretches of hardship, do the kinds of things you know are right: serve your spouse, pray for them, seek counsel, and forgive. Persistence is doing what is right consistently, even when your actions are not appreciated, reciprocated, or even recognized. As Friedrich Nietzsche observes in his book *Beyond Good and Evil*:

> The essential thing "in heaven and in earth" is . . . that there should be long obedience in the same direction, there thereby results, and has always resulted in the long run, something that has made life worth living.

Another key to enduring a long-term crisis of faith is perspective. However long you must endure a crisis of faith, eternity is longer. However great your trial, heavenly reward is greater. However good it might seem to stop believing and put yourself first, knowing God and trusting Him is better. Perspective will keep you going when you feel like giving up.

Perspective is especially hard in a long-term crisis because it feels as though there is no end. Spending time with mature saints is especially helpful in such situations, because they have likely endured long periods of hardship. Mature saints have dealt with seasons of financial hardship, wayward children, marital turmoil, and personal doubt. Having been through it, they can encourage you with needed perspective.

Fourth, a crisis of faith can end suddenly and mysteriously. One day you may feel weak in the faith, and another day you may feel strong. Nothing known to you may explain how the crisis began or how it ended.

Winston Churchill once said on a radio broadcast the actions of the Russian government were "a riddle, wrapped in a mystery inside an enigma; but perhaps there is a key." A crisis of faith can be complicated—a riddle wrapped inside a mystery inside an enigma. However, there are keys to provide escape from Doubting Caste.

We have stressed those keys, including the need for confession, community, and counsel. It should be noted that it can be especially hard to talk to others about a crisis of faith when you cannot explain why you are feeling the way you are feeling. A crisis that results from suffering or scholarship is often more evident to others, relatable, and easy to explain. On the other hand, if you cannot make sense of your own unexplained doubt, it can be intimidating to talk to others.

Do not let this keep you struggling with doubt alone. You should know that mysterious seasons of doubt and unbelief are common. It is likely others in your church, for instance, have experienced times of unexplained spiritual malaise. Just because you cannot explain your crisis of faith does not mean you should not talk to others about your crisis of faith.

Lastly, for some people, a crisis of faith may only end in death. It is possible a season of intense doubt, struggle, suffering, or questioning persists and is never fully resolved *in this life*. People who have lost children, for instance, may experience recurring or persistent doubt, anger, or confusion.

For the believer, death is at once the final crisis and an end to all crisis. Death is a crisis because it is scary and its manner and timing are unknown to us. However, it is the end to all crisis because it ushers the believer into the eternal peace of perfect union with God. Death is the ultimate paradox for the believer, a both dreaded and joyful day.

Whether your crisis ends as the result of action, crisis, time, mystery, or death, you can be sure it will end. These things do not last forever. God will see you through. In the end, faith wins.

Practical Steps

The classic book *Gulliver's Travels* tells the story of a surgeon named Lemuel Gulliver who embarks on epic adventures. On his first journey, Gulliver is shipwrecked on a small island inhabited by miniature people who tie Gulliver down. Since Gulliver is like a giant to the natives, he is bound not by one giant rope but rather by a thousand tiny threads.

In the same way, Christians are bound to Christ and survive a crisis of faith not usually by one big thing but by many little things—a thousand tiny threads. A crisis of faith can start in different ways and end in different ways, and there are practical steps God uses to bind us to Christ:

1. **Start with prayer.** David asked God, "How long?" (Psalm 13:1). John the Baptist asked, "Are you the one?" (Matthew 11:3). In your doubt, go to God. Confess your doubt and unbelief but also declare your faith and the merit of Christ.

   Prayer should be a part of your daily routine when you draw near to God. Consider not only the habit (what you do) of your spiritual disciplines but also the routine (how you do them). Establishing a time, place, and pattern will help you be consistent.

   In times of despair you often do not know what to pray. You can pray the Scriptures. Read a Psalm, and make it your prayer. When Jesus was on the Cross and experiencing the agony of the Father's wrath, He prayed Psalm 22:1, even as He fulfilled its prophecy (Matthew 27:46).

   If, after reading this book, you are not sure whether or not you have truly been saved, then the first thing you want to do is pray and receive Jesus as your Savior. Start by agreeing with God that you are a sinner and are unable to save yourself. Believe that Jesus is the Son of God, who alone can deliver you from sin and death by His sacrifice on the Cross and resurrection on the third day. Regardless of your age or background, if there is any doubt as to whether or not you have been truly saved, start with a prayer of salvation such as this:

God, I know I am a sinner and deserve your wrath. I also know that You are merciful to sinners. I believe that Jesus died on the Cross to pay the penalty of my sins. I receive Him as my Savior and my Lord. I trust in Him, and I commit myself to following Him. He is alive, and I want to be alive in Him. Thank You for saving a sinner like me.

These are true words, but they are not magic words. Merely saying them does not save you, but if you believe the substance of this prayer, then you are saved. There is an empty grave somewhere outside Jerusalem that proves beyond reasonable doubt that God saves sinners who trust in Jesus. If there is any doubt about where you stand with God, pray that prayer (or something like it), and begin a new life with Jesus in a local Bible-believing church.

2. **Go to church.** Since God is triune, He has eternally existed in community—the Father, Son, and Spirit have always had each other. You are made in God's image to exist in community. You need community like a fish needs water. Don't make Elijah's mistake and isolate yourself from the people God intends to use to revive you.

    Find a biblically healthy church and join. Wrap your life in the rhythms of church life. Rather than asking, "What do I like doing?" ask yourself, "What is my church family doing?" If you love Christ, you must love His bride, the church.

3. **Read the Bible.** Rather than focusing on what you don't know and what is out of your control, put your time and energy into knowing God's story of redemption. Nothing will strengthen your faith or preserve your spiritual sanity like God's Word.

4. **Choose to obey.** Start building a life of obedience upon the foundation of salvation, church membership, and daily time in the Word. Put your energy into obedience. You may not feel strong in your faith. You may not even be sure if you still possess faith. You can, however, choose to obey. Never forget the life-changing power of a single decision.

5. **Confess and repent.** Some people think confession and repentance are only done when you get saved. The truth is that the Christian life is one of daily confession and repentance. Confession is admitting your sin to God. The Bible contains a powerful promise: If we confess our sins, He is faithful and just to cleanse us from our sins and to cleanse us from all unrighteousness (1 John 1:9). Since you have ongoing sin, you must have ongoing confession.

    Resist the temptation to make excuses for sin. Excuses only perpetuate a crisis of faith. Calling sin by some other name minimizes its offense to God and in turn strengthens doubt. It is a kind of excuse. Rationalizing sin is not biblical confession.

Simply owning sin as "mess" or "weakness" or "struggle" is not biblical confession. These are ways we subtly undermine the seriousness of sin and pretend to address a problem without actually confessing.

Sin is the enemy of faith. Hate sin, and you will strengthen faith. Once sin is confessed, the next step is repentance, which means to turn away from sin. We inevitably overcomplicate repentance. Think about whatever sin has contributed to your crisis of faith. Turn away from that sin. Tell someone the sin you intend to turn away from in order to establish accountability. Don't overthink this step.

6. **Serve others.** A crisis of faith often makes the world about "me." One way to battle for faith is to serve others. Escape from the prison of self by praying for others, blessing others, giving to others, and serving others. It is better to give than to receive.

Modern Christian culture seems preoccupied with avoiding burnout—being drained of spiritual energy and vitality. The concern seems to be that unless you schedule ample time for yourself (e.g., "me time"), you will grow weary and experience negative spiritual side effects (e.g., despair, hopelessness, etc.).

Thankfully God has established a pattern in creation with a day of rest each week and sleep every night. Following this pattern will provide rest and rejuvenation. Most modern cultures have opportunities for vacations, and taking advantage of these opportunities is both spiritually wise and physically beneficial.

That said, choosing to serve like Jesus means serving out of exhaustion and in hardships. Quite frankly, it means serving others when they should be serving you. Christlike service defies modern culture's obsession with self-care and self-love. Paradoxically, when you feel like being served but choose to serve others, you will find a greater joy and renewed energy.

There is nothing supernatural about serving when it makes sense. The power of the Spirit and the mind of Christ are on display when you serve others who should be serving you. Jesus washed His disciples' feet, but He was the Master! Be wise, but don't worry about burnout. Trust God to keep you going. Choose to serve when others won't.

7. **Share the gospel.** In a crisis of faith, you need to remind yourself of the truth. What better way than telling someone else about the truth? In telling others about the gospel, you will be reminded of the gospel, and whatever their response, you will be blessed.

   It is common for pastors to preach a sermon and then say, "I needed that!" Sharing the gospel is what we need, and telling others is what they need, so a crisis of faith is a perfect time to kill two birds with one stone.

8. **Pursue beauty.** God established a world that declares His glory. Sin makes it ugly, and in a crisis of faith, we tend to see more ugliness than beauty. Beauty builds faith, so if you encounter beauty, it will help to restore your faith.

   There are three kinds of beauty worth pursuing in a crisis of faith: natural beauty, artistic beauty, and moral beauty. Natural beauty is observed in nature. The Bible says the heavens declare the glory of the Lord (Psalm 19:1). Going for a hike, a drive in the country, or a walk in a garden can fill your senses with evidence of God's goodness and presence. Naturalists often call nature their church. While I do not believe nature can take the place of church, I know what they mean. In nature, we encounter evidence of something greater than ourselves. Another opportunity to escape the prison of self.

   Even if you are confined to a hospital bed, you can encounter nature through sounds, images, and books that describe nature. You can listen to nature sounds and almost smell the rain and the thunderstorms. Beauty is God's book too. Like the Bible, Jesus is the main character. The beauty of creation points us to the beauty of the Creator.

   Artistic beauty also has curative powers during a crisis of faith. Find an art gallery and spend time staring at the wonder of human imagination. Man is made in God's image. God is creative, and therefore humans are creative.[2] Art is evidence of

---

[2] God created out of nothing (*ex nihilo*) while humans create out of the material that God has

God's image in humanity, and therefore art is evidence of God's existence.

Take in a sculpture, a symphony, or a guitar solo. Whatever your aesthetic taste, behold the wonder of art, and let your mind be drawn to God. He is the giver of all good things and the source of all beauty. But be careful. "Ugly" art, such as movies, songs, or images that celebrate evil, will worsen a crisis of faith.

Moral beauty is also a source of encouragement during a crisis of faith. Go somewhere to behold charity, and let your heart be warmed. Serve in a homeless shelter, volunteer for a special needs event, or attend a fundraiser for a worthy charity. There is good in the world because God is real. When you encounter goodness you are confronting the reality of God's existence. Your faith will be encouraged, and you will get perspective.

9. **Enjoy life.** All good gifts in life come from God. We honor Him by enjoying His good gifts. Eat good food and fellowship with Christian friends who makes you laugh and think. Enjoy travel, hobbies, exercise, culture, and the arts. Life is bittersweet. You must endure what is bitter and enjoy what is sweet.

   A crisis of faith tricks us into thinking the world is small and options are limited. Seeing the world expands your horizons, your goals, and your dreams. You can escape from the prison of self by seeing the world through travel or just reading a good book. In his famous allegory of the cave, Plato insisted that there was more to life than meets the eyes. He is right. Seeing and enjoying life engages the imagination about things beyond ourselves, greater than ourselves, and the best of ourselves.

10. **Tell your story.** You are going through something, or you've been through something, and other Christians need to hear your testimony. This may be over dinner or coffee with a friend or small group from church. Or you may have an opportunity to share your story with the youth group or senior adults. Your story matters to God, and it matters to His people. How you've

---

created (*ex materia*).

made it this far is a tribute to God's goodness and proof that you can make it through a crisis of faith.

11. **Keep your focus.** In John 21:15–19, Jesus tells Peter to feed His sheep and the kind of death Peter would die. After this, He says, "Follow me" (v. 19). Immediately Peter turns and looks at another disciple and says, "What about this man?" (v. 21). Jesus rebukes Peter and tells him, essentially, to mind his own business (v. 22).

God has given each of us different gifts, challenges, and opportunities. Proverbs 16:33 says, "The lot is cast into the lap, but its every decision is from the Lord." God is good, but He is not fair in the human sense.

Peter was distracted from following Jesus by looking at another person. So often our doubts stem from sinful comparisons. Looking at what other people have (or don't have) and feeling angry at God for not giving us what we think we deserve is a kind of bondage. Jesus tells Peter (and us) to mind our own business, and then He repeats the command with intensity: "You follow me!" (John 21:22).

This book began with a hiking analogy, and it is fitting to end with another. In the hiking community, a common phrase is, "Hike your own hike." Each of us must follow Christ for ourselves. You cannot follow Christ for me, and I cannot follow Christ for you. Paul says in Galatians 6:2 that we must bear one another's burdens. Paradoxically, only a few verses later, Paul says each of us must bear our own burden (v. 5).

In a crisis of faith, remember to hike your own hike. Look to Jesus, and put one foot of faith in front of the other. God's people can help you, but they cannot follow Jesus for you. Keep your focus, and don't be distracted.

Faith Wins

Every genuine Christian will survive their crisis of faith. God will not lose a single one of His children (John 6:35–40). Everyone who trusts in Jesus will make it through their crisis of faith.

This should motivate you to action. Take control of your time, take control of your thoughts, and take control of your actions. Work hard and trust God.

You are never alone. You are never helpless. Life is never out of God's control. There is always hope in Jesus.

Eventually your crisis will end. Until then, be strong in the Lord.

**If you enjoyed this book,
will you consider sharing the message with others?**

Let us know your thoughts at info@newhopepublishers.com.
You can also let the author know by visiting or sharing a photo of the
cover on our social media pages or leaving a review at a retailer's site.
All of it helps us get the message out!

Twitter.com/NewHopeBooks

Facebook.com/NewHopePublishers

Instagram.com/NewHopePublishers

———————————

New Hope® Publishers, Ascender Books, Iron Stream Books, and
New Hope Kidz are imprints of Iron Stream Media,
which derives its name from Proverbs 27:17,
"As iron sharpens iron, so one person sharpens another."

This sharpening describes the process of discipleship, one to
another. With this in mind, Iron Stream Media provides a variety of
solutions for churches, ministry leaders, and nonprofits ranging from
in-depth Bible study curriculum and Christian book publishing to
custom publishing and consultative services. Through the popular
Life Bible Study and Student Life Bible Study brands, ISM provides
web-based full-year and short-term Bible study teaching plans as well
as printed devotionals, Bibles, and discipleship curriculum.

For more information on ISM and New Hope Publishers,
please visit

IronStreamMedia.com

NewHopePublishers.com